IN MY BROTHER'S WORDS

THE MEMOIR OF
Susan Mercogliano

by **CHRIS MERCOGLIANO**

The Oxford Village Press

The Oxford Village Press
P.O. Box 572
Oxford, NY 13830

Cover and book design by Scribe Freelance
www.scribefreelance.com

Library of Congress Cataloging-in-Publication Data
Mercogliano, Chris
In my brother's words by Chris Mercogliano
p.cm.
ISBN 0-945700-08-3
1. Memoir—Disability Rights—History

Library of Congress Control Number

Printed in the United States of America

10 9 8 7 6 5 4 3 2 1

The Oxford Village Press

IN MY BROTHER'S WORDS

THE MEMOIR OF
Susan Mercogliano

Acknowledgments

First and foremost, to the visionary founders of Holly Center for creating such a caring community for people like Susan. And then of course to the dedicated, determined, and loving staff and volunteers for fulfilling the center's mission extraordinarily all these many years. To the leaders and membership of A Voice of Reason for speaking truth to power and giving more and more voice to the voiceless in a time when our government seems to care less and less. To the members of the news media who report on disability issues for keeping us alerted to what's going on. To the legislators and public servants who truly do care for their willingness to swim against the tide and insist that we as a nation do everything possible to address the needs of our most vulnerable citizens. To Mary, Aimee, and Mark for trusting me with their stories. To Lisa, Erin, Connie, and Scottie at Holly Center for helping me paint a more complete portrait of Susan. To Cousin Marie Land for filling in the gaps in our family history. To Hugo Dwyer for helping me understand the bigger picture. To John Taylor Gatto and Oxford Village Press for supporting this unusual project. To my wife

Betsy and my sister Samantha for all their encouragement and editorial assistance. To Tisha Graham for making the manuscript shine. And last but far from least, to my second mom Bunty Ketcham for helping bring Susan's story to light.

Prologue

I still have joy; I still have joy!
After all the things I've been through,
I still have joy!
There were times in my life when I felt I couldn't go on
But the Lord He blessed me and He made me strong.
I kept the faith and I held on through the night.
This is my testimony—that He made everything alright!

—traditional Gospel tune

My brother is telling my story because I can't. An undeveloped frontal lobe made language impossible. Instead, I communicate with a variety of grunts and other guttural sounds. Oh, and I can belly laugh with the best of them. Despite my predicament, there are plenty of times when life is downright hilarious. Then I take great delight in letting you know how amused I am.

Other things came out wrong after a troubled pregnancy and a six-week-early exit from the womb. My right leg ended up several inches shorter than my left. My right arm was similarly undersized and also paralyzed, such that all I've been able to use it for is a kind of clamp to hold stuff. And my eyes are crossed, too, meaning that I have always seen things a bit differently.

Chris, by the way, is just the one to do this for me. Like our mother, he's a writer with a knack for a good tale. Also, only eleven months separate us—Irish twins as they say— and thus we have a great deal in common. We shared many of the same experiences growing up and swam in the same emotional waters, which were often murky at best. So deep down I guess we *are* almost twins. The fact that he already understands how precious every life is and how we all deserve a chance to voice our stories is icing on the cake.

The reason we're so close in age is that our old-fashioned father courted Mom for seven years before he popped the question. Before that was the war and then college at night on the GI Bill. During the day, Daddy worked in a theater showing films. He went on living at home with his mother, determined not to marry until he'd finished law school and landed a good job. When he finally proposed to Mom, he was nearly 34 and in a hurry to make up for lost time. No doubt there would've been more of us if—that part of the story comes later.

The reason Chris is beginning this project as we speak is that I have had fourth-stage cancer for a while now, and my liver is slowly shutting down. I lost all interest in food about a week ago, which means my remaining days are down to a handful or two.

The good news is the liver has no nerve endings, so I'm

not in any pain. Also, Chris and my younger sister Samantha earlier decided for me that, since the cancer was terminal by the time the doctors discovered it, I would skip radiation and chemo in order to continue leading a normal life for as long as possible. Thanks to them, I didn't stop reporting to my job at the Somerset Developmental Center until about ten days ago. I have worked there for the past forty years doing things like putting vending machine trinkets inside plastic capsules and fastening on the caps. I only quit going because I just don't have the energy anymore.

You see, even people as mentally and physically challenged as me take pride in doing purposeful work. I'm not sure everybody understands how important it is to our sense of self, too.

There's more good news: The place called Holly Center, where I have lived for the past 43 years, is like heaven on earth for developmentally disabled people. I share a cottage with a dozen others and have known some of my cottage mates for decades. My caregivers, like Connie who has been here even longer than me, tend to be lifers as well. They see their job as a calling and not a stepping stone to something better. So this is my home, and they are all my family. I'm always treated with the utmost kindness and respect. To the staffers who were raised around here in the southern culture of the Chesapeake Bay's Eastern Shore, instead of Susan, I am affectionately known as Miss Sue-Sue.

I'm also lucky that Holly Center's resident doctor long ago decided that, in order for the center to fulfill its mission entirely, we should be able to die in our own beds. Dr. Waris wants us to be attended to by familiar hands and voices right up to the end. He became a certified hospice physician just to make it possible.

Chris likes to tell people that Bill Gates couldn't buy better care than I get here. I couldn't agree more.

A STEADY STREAM of visitors has been dropping in for the past several days. They kiss me and pet my head and hold my good hand warmly. There have been a lot of tears, too, which I don't quite understand. Frankly, I'm finding the sudden rush of attention a bit confusing. Chris also says it's as though I'm trapped inside a burning building and don't realize it. I suppose he's right once again.

It's not like I haven't been seriously ill before, with three different hospital stints over the years. The first time was to have my bum hip removed after walking around for so long with such an uneven gait. It wore the poor joint down to the bone, and the pain finally became more than I could bear. They had always made wheelchairs available, but I cherished my mobility and still insisted on walking even when it started to hurt like hell. Stubbornness is a family trait, you see.

In case you're wondering why I didn't get a new hip so that I could continue to walk, it's because I wouldn't have been able to do all the rehab exercises that went along with it. Plus ever since I can remember, I have crossed my leg over my knee when I'm sitting down because it's one of the things I could see to do to let people know I'm a woman who values her dignity. But the one thing you *can't* do with an artificial hip is cross your leg over your knee. It dislocates the hip, and then they have to do the surgery all over again.

I found the wheelchair depressing at first, but things brightened back up once I had figured out how to get around by myself by using the foot on my good leg to propel the chair across the floor. My independence has always been paramount, too. It's why so many older people insist on continuing to drive, sometimes long after they should.

The second hospital stay was to have one of my kidneys removed after a monster stone nearly caused it to explode. It had taken Dr. Waris a long time to figure out why I had stopped eating so abruptly and kept scratching my face and grunting more than usual. By then it was too late. But I don't blame him in the least, because it's hard to diagnose someone who can't tell you where it hurts. He's actually quite good at it.

The last time was when my annual physical revealed a malignant tumor lurking in my colon. Once they had removed it, they looked for signs of cancer elsewhere and didn't find any. But a year later it showed up in my liver.

NOW LET ME tell you about purses and handbags, the other way that I express pride in my femininity. I have to have at least one in my clutches *at all times* because to be a proper lady means to have your personal articles immediately at hand, hidden from view in the most stylish way possible. In my case, you won't find lipstick, keys, or a phone inside. Instead, it's always chockablock full of crayons and markers and all my latest artwork, as coloring is my passion and I am quite prolific. You'll also find one of my favorite stuffed animals if the bag is big enough, and maybe an occasional ball.

Size indeed matters. If you want to see me light up when you come to visit, don't bother buying a pricey Gucci or Louis Vuitton. Just bring me something large enough to contain my current selection and still leave room for more stuff. It saves me the hassle of unpacking and repacking—you'd be amazed at how much I can cram into even the daintiest little number.

Something else you should know about me is that I have a bit of a larcenous streak. All sorts of items that don't belong to me have a habit of winding up in my bag. It was especially bad when Cindy was my roommate because she couldn't see what I was doing, and her mom who lived nearby was always bringing her nice things.

That's right, I was literally robbing my best friend blind. Or I guess you could say my blind best friend. But it was okay in the end because my bag is like a safe deposit box for the cottage. When anything goes missing, the staff knows exactly where to find it. And your valuables are always secure with me because no purse snatcher, no matter how determined, is ever going to separate me from my most prized possession. Though well under 100 pounds soaking wet, I'm still strong as an ox.

Just ask Chris and Samantha about the time they took me to the Holly Center thrift store to get me a new handbag. "Store" is a misnomer in this case because you don't have to pay for any of the merchandise. That day there was a whole bin full of pocketbooks and purses, and so I dove in like a woman possessed. I had a firm grip on at least a dozen before they knew what had hit them. They made a noble effort to pry some of them loose, but I'll be damned. This was a once-in-a-lifetime jackpot. Besides, they were FREE! Just as they were about to call out to one of the staff for backup, we settled out of court on three. Still not a bad day's haul.

Or there was that little fiasco with the therapeutic ball bath. It's an inflatable pool filled with hard, brightly colored plastic balls that Somerset had just bought for clients who need more sensory stimulation. I had no urge whatsoever to get in it, but I sure thought those little balls were cool. So cool that when nobody was looking, I decided to slip a few into my purse every day and take them home.

Connie noticed the booty I kept bringing back from work but thought little of it at first. Thankfully she had the instinct to save the balls every time I took them out of my bag to make room for other stuff because one day, a couple of weeks later, someone from Somerset phoned Holly Center to ask about them. "This may sound silly," the woman said, "but almost all the balls from our new therapy bath have gone missing, and we can't seem to find them anywhere. You haven't seen any floating around there, have you?"

Connie almost died laughing when she heard about it. Once she had recovered, she called the woman at Somerset back to say that she sure had seen the balls. Three trash bags full! Then Connie ratted me out—kindly of course—and they shared a good chuckle. The cache of stolen balls was on the bus to Somerset with me the next morning, and the room with the therapy bath was off-limits after that. `

AS FOR DOCTORS and hospitals, life had more or less returned to normal the other times they worked on me and gave me medicine. Thus it's hard to wrap my mind around something else happening this time. Is my lack of awareness about my current situation more good news? I'm not sure of the answer.

My reality has always been confined to this moment, which I guess is a blessing and a curse. Some people get stuck in the past; others are constantly worrying about the future. They both have to go to great lengths to learn how to be present in the here and now. Me, that's all I know. But being unable to refer to the past or anticipate the future forecloses so many possibilities. It makes it impossible to invent the life you imagine for yourself.

It's a little like playing blackjack in a casino. Most people, if they don't like the way the cards are falling, will pick up their chips and move to a different table instead. But I've never had that option. I was dealt the hand I was dealt, and I'm still playing with the same cards. There was never anything I could do on my own to change my luck.

But it hasn't kept me from living a life that is fully human, filled with triumphs, and tragedies, and everything in between.

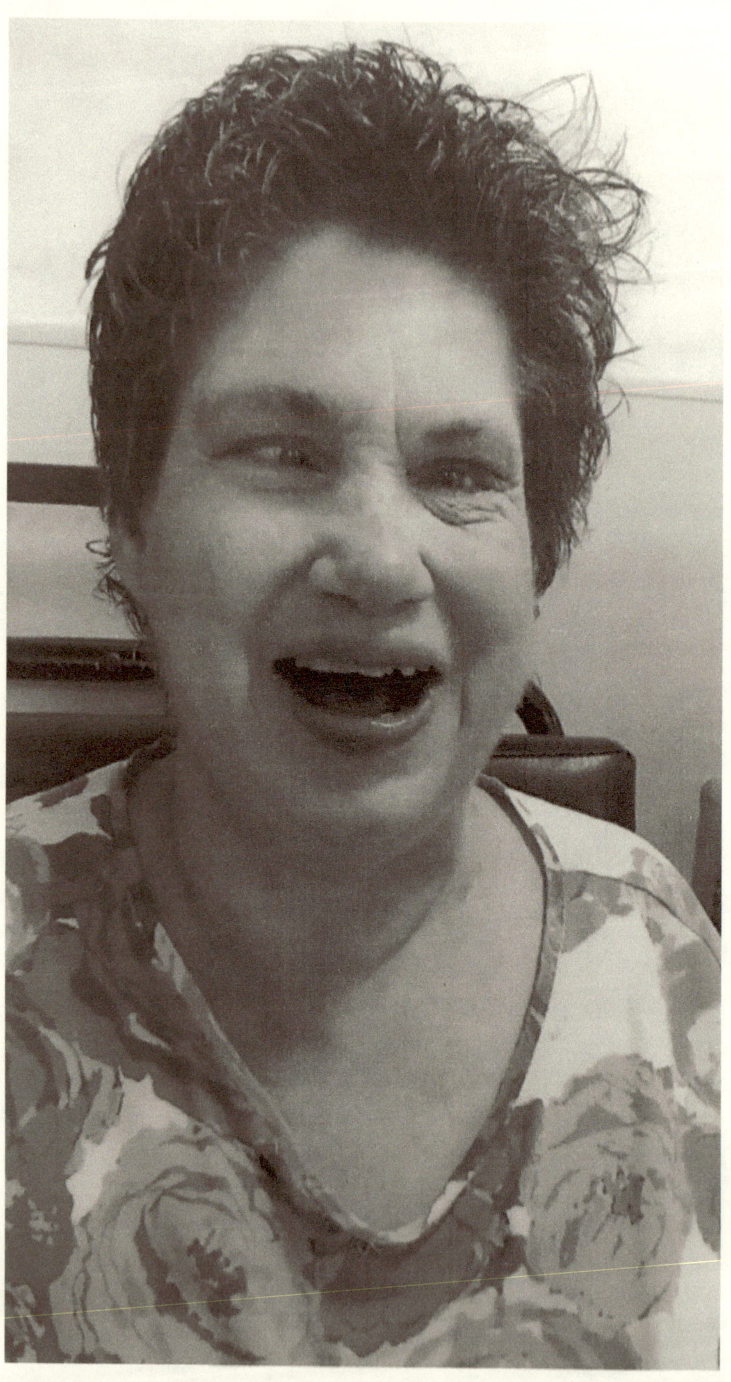

ONE

I was born on April 5, 1955. Dwight Eisenhower was president, and it was the year the Pentagon started building nuclear missiles. To balance the ledger, Walt Disney came out with the Mickey Mouse Club, which my brothers and I watched together religiously. 1955 was also when Rosa Parks got arrested for refusing to give up her bus seat to a white person, and when Ray Kroc opened the first McDonald's. A gallon of gas cost 23 cents.

My parents were Charles and Carol Mercogliano. Our last name signals that my father's people originated in a town by the same name on the forested slopes above Naples. Many family members have visited Mercogliano at one time or another, and pretty much everyone has come back saying that the only thing going for it is a beautiful monastery perched on top of the mountain into which artisans first carved their houses back in Roman times.

My father's father came over on the boat all by himself when he was eleven, with only a satchel of clothes in one hand. I have no idea how he managed once he got to New York City, but as you will see as my story unfolds, resilience seems to run in the family, too. Angelo settled in Brooklyn and became a barber. In the few photos that remain of him, he is always fashionably dressed.

Grandpa, long dead before I came along, somehow met my grandma Lillie, whose parents had left Italy a generation earlier. The Riccis hailed from the Isle of Capri, where rumor has it my great-great-grandfather dove for pearls.

Grandma Merc was probably the most resilient of us all; although on second thought, my other grandmother could've given her a run for her money. I'll tell you about Grandma Poff in a moment.

While Grandma Merc was twelve and living somewhere in Brooklyn with her mother and father and six brothers and sisters, her mother—for reasons unknown—jumped to her death from a top-floor window. Then Grandma's father just took off one day soon after, apparently back to Italy where he married a younger woman. Because Grandma was the oldest daughter, she suddenly found herself head of the household. I have no idea how she managed either. The suicide became a family secret, and none of us who are still around know much about this dark chapter in our history.

At some point, Grandma and Grandpa got married. Grandma was working as a seamstress at the time and sewed herself the most beautiful wedding gown you've ever seen. Chris has a framed picture of it that our cousin Marie gave us. Then they moved to Washington, DC, where my dad and his two brothers were born and raised in the old Italian neighborhood in the city's northeast quadrant.

My mom, even though she was German and Scotch-

Irish, finished growing up in the same neighborhood. It's where she and Daddy met.

Mom's people had all settled in the coal mining hills of West Virginia, which is where her mother became the first female postal carrier east of the Mississippi River. Chris says the reason for the distinction is that there had apparently been a female Pony Express rider out west back in the 1860s.

Grandma Poff, as the story goes, was careful to only put her first initial on the job application and not spell out Alma. Then acing the Postal Service exam earned her a position delivering mail on horseback up where they lived.

But when she arrived for her first day of work, the postmaster immediately waggled his head from side to side. "We never hired no women 'round here, Miss Poff, and we ain't about to start now."

Which was the wrong thing to say to my grandmother. She went straight to her congressman in Charleston and demanded that he intercede on her behalf. What choice did he have? There she was the next day, riding a horse with two saddlebags full of U.S. mail.

Somewhere along the way, Grandma got married and had six kids. Then the Great Depression hit them like a brick. After Grandpa lost his job along with everyone else in those parts, his only option was to shoehorn Grandma and the kids into their old Ford sedan with a loaf of bread and a couple of pounds of baloney and cruise around the Midwest looking for work. With none to be found, he and Grandma started dropping the children off one by one at friendly farms that could afford to feed them in exchange for a little work. Mom wound up somewhere out in Indiana.

Grandpa eventually became a hobo riding the rails and eventually disappeared altogether. When the Depression ended, Grandma moved to DC and somehow landed a job as a secretary in the Commerce Department. After she had banked enough cash and found a big enough apartment, she sent for the kids so that they could be a family again.

You see what I mean about Grandma Poff being one tough cookie, too, not to be trifled with? When she retired many years later, the first thing she did was take a trip around the world—all by herself! She decided upon her return to move into a little house trailer on a canal somewhere down in Florida. That's how determined she was to get away from her now-grown children who were always feuding with each other over one silly thing or another. Mom and my Aunt Patty, who lived across town from us, would go years without speaking. Having originated in Hatfield and McCoy country had left an indelible mark.

I would never see Grandma, who babysat me a lot when I was little, again.

AFTER MY MOM and dad were married, they bought a sweet new house on a one-acre lot just past the first ring of Maryland suburbs that were beginning to sprout up outside DC. We were about five miles beyond the future Beltway, which wouldn't exist for another ten years. Daddy was an attorney with the IRS and earning a good salary, making this their American Dream home. The neighbors across the road had a big white horse, and Paint Branch was the rear boundary of our property as it snaked its way toward the Anacostia River. Creeks are known as "branches" around there, and the hamlet we were in is called Paint Branch Farms.

Chris, when he got a little older, would spend most of his time playing in the creek with our big brother. Johnnie was eight when I was born. Technically he was a half-brother because at age 20 Mom had a short-lived first marriage to another Italian guy, a meat cutter from Pittsburgh. But the son of a bitch started knocking her around when she was eight months pregnant, so she wisely dumped him and moved back in with her mother.

Sadly, Johnnie never got to know his father. It would turn out to be just the first in a series of childhood bad breaks.

But for now, Daddy was a dream dad. When he graduated number one in his class from GW law school, he received a bunch of big offers from oil companies in Houston and Dallas. He turned them all down because more than anything else he wanted to raise a passel of children. So instead he chose a nine-to-five government job that would make it possible to always be there for us. And was he ever. Every day when he got home from work at 5:20 sharp, the first thing he would do was throw me up and down in his arms and call me his Susannah Francesca.

It didn't matter that I wasn't all there; he said I was his little angel.

As for Johnnie, the first thing Daddy did after marrying Mom was to legally adopt him. Daddy wanted there to be no doubt in Johnnie's mind just how he felt about being his father.

Not everything came up roses after I was born. What all parents want more than anything else is for their babies to come out whole, and I obviously wasn't. On some level that they never allowed me to see, they were heartbroken at first. Then there was all the anxious waiting and hoping against hope—was I going to be mentally disabled too?

At six months, Mom noticed my inability to track objects. I was also slow to start reaching for rattles and toys and didn't begin to crawl for well over a year. Walking didn't come until three and a half. And speech, of course, never materialized at all.

However, if not for my turned-in eyes, above the shoulders I resembled a perfectly normal girl. I was quite pretty as a matter of fact, with thick, dark hair and brown eyes with long lashes. I looked a lot like my Grandma Merc when she was a young, southern Italian beauty. In that wedding portrait I mentioned, she's a real stunner. Today, Chris says, I look more like her than ever.

ONCE IT WAS certain I would never be like other children, my parents were able to exhale and regroup. We relaxed into a life that looked a lot like other families. Daddy drove off to work every morning. Johnnie hopped on a big yellow school bus. Chris and I stayed home with Mom. She was an avid gardener, and pretty soon the house was surrounded by dogwoods, azaleas, and all kinds of colorful annuals and perennials. Daddy mowed the lawn on weekends.

Chris and I played together in the morning while Mom

gardened or did housework. We had a Collie named Sam to keep us company, and some days Mom would have a friend or a neighbor over for coffee. Then after lunch, Chris and I watched Mom's soap operas with her. We knew it was time for our nap when *As the World Turns* came on at 1:30. Talk about resilient—CBS continued to make that show until 2010. How did they ever come up with enough material for over 10,000 episodes?

Mom had converted to Catholicism before she married Daddy, and so on Sunday mornings the five of us went to Mass together. Then Mom would fix something special for an early supper, while Daddy whipped up a homemade dessert. They were both very good cooks, and I have always loved to eat as a result. It's no wonder that among all the deficiencies listed in my childhood medical evaluations, they also noted how adept I was at feeding myself. Followed by the critical addition that I was overly fond of making meals a social event. Haha.

With almost all the Mercs and Riccis living in the area, too, Johnnie, Chris, and I were surrounded by a large and demonstrative extended family. Grandma and my aunts and uncles rallied around Mom and Daddy to help make me feel loved and accepted. At family parties, which happened with great frequency, there was always a big poker game where the grown-ups sat around the dining room table drinking Manhattans and beer out of a can. My cousins would watch eagerly over their shoulders, hoping for a chance to play a hand or two when somebody got up to pee.

And *mamma mia*, the feasts we would have! Every

Fourth of July my uncles went down to the wharf to buy five-dollar bushels of blue crabs. Then they lined up picnic tables in Aunt Pat and Uncle Vic's backyard and covered them with newspaper so that we could sit and pick crabs all day until it was time for the neighborhood parade. Uncle Vic was Daddy's younger brother and Chris's godfather. At Thanksgiving, Christmas, and Easter, there was antipasto; turkey, roast beef, or lamb; and always a big pasta dish of some sort or another. Grandma Merc's lasagna was to die for.

Family weddings especially were a hoot. The kids ran around having at least as much fun as the grown-ups, while I took it all in from a perch in Daddy's or one of my uncle's strong arms.

Life was good for a time.

TWO

Things went to hell in a hurry after Daddy's diagnosis. He had been a heavy smoker, preferring unfiltered Chesterfields to Mom's Winstons. And there was almost no hope for him because in those days the only available treatment was a surgeon hacking away at the cancerous tissue in his throat to temporarily stave off the inevitable.

I was two and change.

When Daddy went in for the first of a series of operations, the joy rushed out of our lives like the air from a burst balloon. The first time he recovered fairly fast, and a semblance of normalcy returned once he was able to go back to work. John still went to school. Mom took care of the house and the garden. Chris and I played and then napped while Mom watched her soaps.

The Mercs and Riccis all prayed for a miracle.

Each successive surgery further sapped Daddy's strength, but not his will. He had three kids to take care of and was determined to finish what he had started. Then, when there was nothing left that the doctors could safely remove, he and Mom played the only card left: a trip to Lourdes in search of divine intervention. Daddy's life was in God's hands for sure, so they boarded an ocean liner and steamed off to France.

Grandma Merc moved in with us to hold down the fort while they were gone. She had been growing increasingly anxious as she got older, which had necessitated her living with Aunt Pat and Uncle Vic. Today Grandma would've been diagnosed with PTSD from the trauma caused by having so much responsibility thrust upon her at such an early age. But back then people just said, "Lillie worries a lot." It didn't help that now she was facing the reality of one of her sons being terminally ill.

Grandma struggled to keep it all together, until one day a couple of neighborhood boys started throwing rocks at Sam to get him to bark. Yelling at them to stop got Grandma nowhere, and the barking became more than she could bear. Afraid that Sam might break loose and bite the boys, she called the dogcatcher, who rushed over and took Sam to the pound.

As soon as Mom and Daddy got back from France, they went straight to bail Sam out. But it had been too long—the pound had already put him down.

We had gotten Sam as a puppy right after Chris was born, and Sam had been growing up right alongside us. So it was a bitter loss. Maybe it was a warning signal, too, like the alarm that goes off on the instrument panel of a 747 when it's losing too much altitude.

Daddy's miracle never came. With the cancer spreading everywhere, his handsome, olive complexion turned the color of ash. He grew so thin you could see his bones, and he must've been in a great deal of pain because Mom was always reminding us to be as quiet in the house as we possibly could.

STILL, DADDY HUNG on and refused to die. Having piloted landing craft in several South Pacific invasions, he wasn't afraid of a good fight. But his personal war was not to be won. A sandlot football star before he joined the Coast Guard, Daddy watched his beloved Navy team beat Army one last time and then surrendered sometime during the night. The doctors said he weighed less than 70 pounds.

Chris had come into their bedroom at first light and was the first to discover Daddy gone. When Mom turned over and saw Chris standing there holding his hand, she knew right away what had happened because Daddy hadn't awakened her for his middle-of-the-night morphine.

Chris wondered why Daddy was so cold.

Mom immediately got up, ushered Chris back to the boys' bedroom, and called the coroner.

No one had ever told Johnnie, Chris, and me that Daddy was so sick he wouldn't get better. There was just more hoping against hope. I'm not sure about Johnnie, who was then 11, but Chris and I were as confused as I am right now. Suddenly Daddy just wasn't there anymore.

Death and dying were still in the closet in those days. You simply didn't talk about it, especially with kids. On the morning of the funeral, Mom sent Chris and me to a neighbor's house down the road for the day.

Interestingly, all of a sudden Chris began behaving a lot

like me. He stopped speaking and retreated into a world of his own. Mom got so worried she called our pediatrician, who told her that Chris was in shock. Dr. Sartwell said Mom needed to confront him with the truth: Daddy was dead, which meant he wasn't coming back. Not ever. She wound up having to hold Chris and shake him by the shoulders, too, until the dam finally broke and tears came flooding out of him.

He started talking again after that.

JOHNNIE, CHRIS, AND I felt devastated for I can't remember how long. Daddy had been our whole world. There's an old black and white photo of us opening Christmas presents a month later, which Mom must've taken, and in it we look like orphans who've just been liberated from a concentration camp. Instead of the gleeful faces you'd expect to see with all those toys and games scattered around a gaily decorated tree, there are three sets of expressionless eyes staring blankly at the camera.

Clearly, we were *still* in shock.

This time there was no normal to return to. Our savings soon ran out, and with only a high school diploma Mom somehow managed to obtain a real estate license and start selling houses. But there was no way she could earn enough right away to keep up with our mortgage, so all in one motion she had to unload the house, move us into a rental nearby enough for Johnnie to stay in the same school, and go to work full time.

The real salt in the wound was that back then there were almost no support services for children like me. Mom's only option was to hire a "housekeeper," whose real purpose was to see to my needs during the day. The first was a woman as old as my grandmothers, and far sterner than they ever were. No one remembers her name.

It seemed like forever before Mom would finally get home from work. When she did she was usually exhausted. She began drinking, though not heavily yet. The new house wasn't nearly as nice as our old one and didn't feel like home at all. There were no fathers, no horses, no creeks, and when Mom got us another dog, he kept breaking loose and killing the neighbors' cats. So Buddy had to be put down, too.

It's enough to make you wonder how there can possibly be a God.

Mom caught somewhat of a break when she got hired as a sales agent in a big cul-de-sac subdivision that was under construction just off New Hampshire Ave., right next to the future I-495. The only finished houses were in a row of model homes at the center of the development, and one of the perks of the job was getting to live in one for free. The houses were a new suburban phenomenon called "split-level homes." Ours was quite stylish inside and Mom loved showing it off to our aunts and uncles and cousins. One of the other models even had an indoor pool. Better still, the sales office was right down the street, meaning that Mom was around a lot more. She seemed much less stressed.

The best thing may've been that our old crone of a housekeeper didn't accompany us. Instead, Mom hired a red-headed young gal who had just come over from Ireland. Bernadette had bouncy energy and a lovely, lilting accent. She liked to sing, and play with me, and make me laugh. When she discovered how much I loved music, she got out Mom and Daddy's albums and dusted off the record player, which hadn't been used in a while. I fancied the silky tenor of Andy Williams most of all, and so she played his stuff over and over for me. Andy had great staying power, too; he only died a few years ago.

Bernadette moved in with us so that some nights Mom could go out. Johnnie was still able to attend the same school, and Chris went to half-day kindergarten at a newly built one close enough for him to walk. I stayed home with Bernadette.

Johnnie and Chris were thrilled with our new neighborhood because houses were being built all around us, which meant dirt mountains to climb, mud holes to muck about in, and lots of scrap lumber for tree forts. The carpenters even supplied the nails. They also boxed up their returnable bottles, and every few days Chris would wheel around his trusty red wagon and collect them. He used the deposits to acquire an impressive collection of baseball cards for a boy his age.

Unbeknownst to my brothers and me, the reason Mom was leaving the house after dinner was to date her boss, the lead broker for the development. We wouldn't meet him for the first time until after we moved yet again two years later.

MOM DECIDED TO relocate us inside DC proper when I

turned six so that I could attend the Sharpe Health School, a special public school for disabled children on 13th St. She used her real estate savvy to buy a beautiful house on the corner of 42nd St. and Military Rd. It had once belonged to a former ambassador to Japan, and I have no idea how Mom managed to get it at a price we could afford. It helped that she had also landed a civil service job as the secretary for a researcher at NIH. Smart like Daddy, before long she was also writing Dr. Klieger's grants. She became his right-hand woman and rose through the pay grades quickly.

Off to school I headed in the Fall of '61, just like Johnnie and Chris. In their case, they both walked to their new schools—Johnnie was in junior high now—while Mom drove me downtown to mine. There weren't any short buses for special needs kids yet. At the risk of repeating myself, somehow she managed to shuttle me to and from school and also get back and forth from NIH in Bethesda every day. There was all that traffic to contend with, and we didn't have the best car in the world. On particularly cold mornings, it often wouldn't start.

I had no real concept of school, of course, but I knew that my brothers were going somewhere important every morning, and now so was I. It was very exciting; I looked forward to it every day.

Little did I know that my career at Sharpe would be so short-lived, however. In November, about the same time of year Daddy had died, the principal called Mom in for a conference. "I'm very sorry, Mrs. Mercogliano," she said, "but your daughter's retardation is just too severe for us to handle."

Or as the school district put it in an extremely terse letter of dismissal, "It has been determined by the staff that Susan has not made the adjustment to our school program that we had hoped."

In other words, somehow they *couldn't* manage. So much for the principal being your pal.

When the local schools can't meet the educational needs of a child residing in the district today, they have to pay for a private alternative. But not in the early '60s. My only option was to stay home again with yet another "housekeeper." This time it was a Black woman in her thirties named Shirley. She was nice to me and could cook pretty well, but she wasn't nearly as much fun as Bernadette. Mostly there were just long hours staring at the TV and waiting for Johnnie, Chris, and Mom to come home.

Not only had the move into the city proved all for naught, it also meant we didn't get to see the Mercs and the Riccis as often because by then most of them had moved to the Maryland suburbs as we had done. Sometimes we would get together with Aunt Patty and my cousins Jimmy, Danny, and Tricia, depending on whether the two mothers were on speaking terms.

Shirley also moved in with us so that Mom could keep seeing the invisible man who was no longer her boss. Once Johnnie, Chris, and I finally did meet him, we soon wished we hadn't. Fred—Mr. Shulley to the three of us—said all the right things, but underneath the façade we could sense how much he disliked kids. The fact, also unbeknownst to us at the time, that he had recently abandoned a wife and child in Pennsylvania where he was born confirmed our instincts. Right around our age, Fred's daughter Nancy wouldn't cross paths with her father again until my younger sister Samantha's wedding many years later. Fred never sent his ex-wife a dime.

There I go leaping ahead again.

Then Fred moved in, too. I suppose it was a fair trade at first because Mom was madly in love with him and happier than she'd been in a long time. Plus after Fred had completed the housing development project, he went into business for himself and was doing pretty well. His and Mom's combined incomes left us flush for a change.

Everything went their way in the beginning. One night they came back from the race track in Charles Town in the middle of the night with their pockets stuffed full of twenties and fifties and hundreds. They had hit practically every daily double and trifecta, and when they added it all up, it amounted to nearly ten grand. No longer with time to garden, Mom used some of the money to pay a landscaper to redo the plantings around the house.

But this stroke of good fortune would prove to be another warning signal. It turned out that Fred conducted his real estate operation like a riverboat gambler who likes to leave all his chips on the table after a big hand. In Fred's case he would immediately double down on some new development scheme, and because the idea was often impulsive and poorly thought through, in the end he would lose everything. That left only Mom's income to get by on, and furthermore they had fallen into the habit of living beyond their means.

Already a heavy drinker, Fred quickly spun out of control

when he was down on his luck. Mom, meanwhile, had started drinking with him. After work they would closet themselves inside Fred's home office for hours on end, knocking down one Schlitz after another. Then the bickering began, and Fred would wind up wallowing in a nightly sea of self-pity.

I CAN'T REMEMBER how long it was before Mom and Fred got married. They didn't tell us until *after* they came home from the justice of the peace. And there never was any party. Johnnie and Chris were beside themselves, having been hoping against hope that Mom would realize her mistake and send this guy packing, too.

The emotional turmoil began to take its toll on me. I started throwing tantrums and hitting myself in the head with my good fist whenever I got upset. Or sometimes I would yank the mattress off my bed, tip over the frame, which was not light, and slam it repeatedly against the wall. Or I meticulously smeared shit on every surface in my room.

Worse still, everyone was attributing these behaviors to the brain damage that was keeping me from being able to form words, construct thoughts, and live a life of my choosing. No one seemed to understand that while I was so mentally different, emotionally I was just like everyone else. Maybe I couldn't verbalize my feelings, but I certainly could *feel* them. And damn it, they had the same rational causes as anyone with a perfectly formed brain.

Sure I was retarded, to use the terminology of the times, but I wasn't crazy. Who wouldn't be grief-stricken and confused after their soft and maternal dad died when they were only three and a half and just learning to walk?

Who wouldn't feel maddeningly frustrated when they couldn't ask questions about what was happening around them and use language to communicate their wants and needs?

Who wouldn't be frightened by the constant dislocations and the increasingly fragile state of their mom's mental health?

Who wouldn't become enraged at being left in the hands of strangers who were often insensitive and sometimes unkind, and at being kicked out of school at age six because they required too much care? And then at their mother for falling in love with an alcoholic, jealous of the attention she paid to her children, and who wanted her all to himself?

It didn't help that Mom wasn't much of a nurturer. But it's no wonder. Who was there to hug and hold her when she got dropped off with people she didn't know and was left to doubt whether she would ever see her mother again? No, Mom was a survivor, descended from a long line of survivors who could take life's punches and still get up and go to work the next morning, or feed the kids breakfast—or both.

Then there was the fact that I had no way to escape the turmoil, not even for a second. My brothers were free to venture outside practically whenever they wanted, to make friends, build forts, play ball, and shoplift candy at the corner store. Later they would be able to sneak Mom's cigarettes and break into Fred's scotch, which disappeared so fast anyway that he never caught on.

What outlets were available to me?

I guess I've been trapped inside a burning building pretty much since day one.

So who, under similar circumstances, wouldn't wind up smashing their bedroom walls and soiling their own nest?

THREE

It is perhaps my generation's most iconic question: Where were you when JFK was assassinated? In my case, the answer was at home on 42nd St. with Shirley. John was in school that awful morning. Chris would've been, too, except for some reason Mom had taken him to see Dr. Sartwell. Instead of bringing him to school after that, Mom decided to drop in on Aunt Pat.

My aunt was sitting in front of her television set crying. She filled Mom in on what had just gone down in Dallas, and then Chris and Mom spent the afternoon with her waiting to see if the President would somehow pull through. Yeah, more hoping against hope.

There I was living in one of the epicenters of world events and yet oblivious to them all. Even though I'll never understand who President Kennedy was, his life still had an enormous impact on mine. Just not for the usual reasons. Most people's takeaway from the assassination had to do with all the what-might-have-beens. JFK was working on so many major issues when his life got cut short—outlawing racial discrimination, getting us out of Vietnam, reining in a rogue

CIA; the list goes on. It would take the next president to accomplish the first initiative, the one after him to complete the second, and then the CIA is still out of control, according to Chris.

What many people don't realize is that something President Kennedy *did* manage to accomplish before he died was to convince Congress to step up to the plate and fund ways to help the developmentally disabled and the mentally ill. Until that time the severely mentally ill mostly ended up in huge, prison-like institutions euphemistically called "state hospitals," which before that were better known as insane asylums. Little was done to help people get better in those terrible places. They were simply watched over, clothed, and fed—often minimally at best.

The same fate awaited people like me with such serious developmental problems that we can't manage on our own either. And actually, many of us with the potential to live independently got stuck in state hospitals anyway. But we'll get to that in a minute. The developmentally disabled were placed on the *back* wards, out of sight and out of mind, where they usually received even less care than the psychiatric "patients." "Inmate" is probably a better word.

In addition the government established a panel of scientists to study the causes of mental illness and developmental disabilities, as well as to explore ways to prevent them from occurring in the first place. After that they set up special research centers to continue the work.

Some of the new funding was earmarked for the creation of much smaller alternatives to state hospitals, ones that would be more integrated into the community. Today they're called Intermediate Care Facilities, or ICFs. In the case of mentally ill people, the emphasis is on ways to help them get better. The goal for the developmentally disabled is to teach us the skills that will enable us to live less restrictively, maybe even out in the mainstream.

This was the point at which government agencies started providing support services to make it possible to care for disabled family members at home. It marked the birth of "special education," too, as school systems began hiring specially trained teachers to work with developmentally disabled children. That way we could go to school every day just like other kids and learn to overcome some of our challenges.

Not that it did me any good.

A lot of people also don't understand why JFK made helping us one of his first priorities. It was because his older sister Rosemary had been born with a damaged brain just like me. Hers wasn't nearly as messed up, but it was enough to keep her from living a normal life, too.

The president had such a wonderful way with words. Here is how he put his intention to make our lives better: "It was said, in an earlier age, that the mind of a man is a far country which can neither be approached nor explored. But, today, under present conditions of scientific achievement, it will be possible for a nation as rich in human and material resources as ours to make the remote reaches of the mind accessible. The mentally ill and the mentally retarded need no longer be alien to our affections or beyond the help of our communities."

Amen.

Another thing people often don't realize is that a lot of other Kennedys got involved in the cause. While he was a U.S. senator from New York in 1965, JFK's younger brother Robert toured the Willowbrook State School, which at the time housed over 6,000 young people. Located in New York City, it was the world's largest institution for the developmentally disabled. Wouldn't you know it had originally been used as a prisoner-of-war camp during WWII?

RFK was so shocked by what he saw that he told reporters the residents were "living in filth and dirt, their clothing in rags, in rooms less comfortable and cheerful than the cages in which we put animals in a zoo." He later called Willowbrook a "snake pit," a comment that attracted national attention. It would take another ten years, but the state eventually shut Willowbrook down.

I know I'm getting ahead of myself again when I say that this is the kind of place I was probably destined for if it weren't for the Kennedys.

MOM AND FRED'S metaphorical honeymoon didn't last long because his boom-or-bust business style and their shared alcoholism kept our household in perpetual chaos. At one point his blood pressure got so high that he was a stroke waiting to happen. When he was broke and had no new deals in the works, he would sit in his office day and night, mired in a complete funk. He wasn't a mean drunk, thank God. But being around a depressed one can be almost as bad.

Then Samantha arrived on the scene the year I turned nine. We sure weren't your typical fifties family anymore, with four kids by three different fathers and seventeen years separating the youngest from the oldest. Topped off by one of us drooling half the time and smacking herself upside the head when she got really mad.

Even though Mom was then forty and had bled much of the way through this pregnancy as well, Sam somehow managed to be born with all her fingers and toes. Along with a headful of the most amazing red hair you'll ever see. It must've been Mom's Irish leaking through.

I couldn't grasp the concept of babies very well and had no idea what to do with one, but Sam sure was fun to watch. Way more interesting than television. There's no memory of my feeling particularly jealous of all the attention Mom was paying to her—I just coveted Sam's stuff. Despite the large age difference, we liked all the same things. Sam still has fuzzy early memories of me raiding her possessions. And back then, they didn't just go into a purse for safekeeping; I wanted them to be permanently mine. My handbag fetish wouldn't blossom until years later.

No one will ever know whether it was my shit-smearing or there just being too many dependent kids in the house that resulted in Fred not wanting me around anymore. He's no longer available for comment. So when Sam had just turned one, Mom and Fred finally found—after two more failed attempts—a school that *could* manage my tantrums and my needs. It was a residential school in Leesburg called the Corley School.

I'm not sure I particularly liked it, but I found a certain measure of comfort in the consistent routines. Plus there was no more uproar swirling around my head all the time. The staff at Corley worked with me on bathroom, bathing, and grooming skills, which I greatly appreciated. It was so important to me to be able to take care of myself, and as far as I know there were never any complaints about my behavior. Hopefully, they weren't drugging me into submission.

I missed Mom and my siblings a lot, but maybe it was just as well this way. Mom's work was important to her, not only for the money. Her office was researching cancer and heart disease, and she was a valuable member of the team. For me to remain at home, sooner or later she would've had to quit because hiring one temporary housekeeper after another to take care of me wasn't a sustainable solution.

Besides, it was lonely at home with Johnnie and Chris hardly ever around anymore. Their way of coping with the turmoil was always to be somewhere else. Both of them practically had second homes at other kids' houses.

AS FOR SAM, this time Fred didn't cut and run. He took being her dad to heart and even played with her once in a while. A drill instructor in the Army Airborne during the war, Fred invented a game for his three-year-old called Jump Out the Plane. After he'd had a few, he would set up a stepladder in the living room and take Sam through the paratrooper pre-jump checklist as she slowly climbed up the rungs.

"One okay, Corporal?" Fred would shout out.

"One okay, sir!" she'd holler back.

And so on until they reached ten.

Then he would yell "JUMP!" and Sam would leap off the top of the ladder into his waiting arms. It was ridiculously cute.

But Johnnie—now John—and Fred didn't get along at all. Between Fred not trying very hard and John already having been burned twice in the father department, their relationship never stood a chance. And by now the turmoil was taking its toll on John, too. He started doing delinquent stuff like skipping school and stealing hubcaps. Then one night he "borrowed" Fred's new Buick without permission—or a driver's license either—and a policeman brought him home at 2:00 a.m.

When it came time for John to graduate from high school, he didn't. He had flunked twelfth grade, and so Fred convinced Mom to send John to a military academy in upstate New York to "straighten him out."

Ironically, it worked. John did pretty well academically, joined the football team, and graduated as an officer. He also got accepted into Fordham.

Chris, meanwhile, took the opposite tack. He was the classic "good boy"—straight A's in school, altar boy at church—and never in any real trouble. Or at least he never got caught because he was sneakier than John and could fool people with that choir-boy face. Then again he wet the bed until he was twelve, which just goes to show how deceiving appearances can be.

What about Mom? On one hand, my absence eliminated

a major flashpoint between Fred and her. It also meant she didn't have to keep trying to find people willing to take care of me for domestic help wages. Locating good help was no small feat—Mom had to fire Shirley's replacement after Mom caught her stealing jewelry.

On the other hand, Mom's relief came at a price. She felt painfully ambivalent about caving into Fred and sending me away, and her guilt would only fester as time went on.

Fred? He had gotten on another roll while I was away at school, such as it was. Suddenly they could also afford to send Chris to an exclusive Jesuit prep school and Samantha, when she turned six, to an equally exclusive school for girls.

But as was usually the case, Fred's dice didn't stay hot for long. This time he had come up with a truly groundbreaking idea, one which would land him on the front page of the Washington Post business section. He had decided to buy a large, run-down apartment complex in the inner city, fix up the apartments, and then sell them to low-income buyers.

Condos for poor people were a brand-new concept, and the Federal Housing Administration agreed to subsidize people's mortgages. It was sure to be a winner. So Fred invested all the cash he had on hand and also borrowed millions more from a big DC bank, on the condition that a certain percentage of units sold by a certain date.

But vandalism was a constant problem, delaying renovations, and fear of the neighborhood slowed down sales. Even though Fred came extremely close to meeting the deadline, the bank foreclosed on the loan anyway. He then sued them and lost, which left him with a hefty legal bill on top of everything else.

Busted again, Fred was unable to keep paying our tuition. Mom's income was only enough to cover basic expenses, and so Sam and I both had to leave our schools. Chris's allowed him to stay because he was a good student and well-liked by his teachers and the headmaster. They made up a work scholarship for him, which entailed him cleaning the school chapel every Saturday. John had decided to drop out of Fordham anyway so that he could pursue his passion for music. In high school he had taught himself to play the drums and the guitar and would soon go on to organize a popular band here on the Eastern Shore.

As for me, I was now fourteen and homeless.

My living at 42nd St. no longer an option, as a last resort Mom had me admitted to Washington's Hospital for Sick Children for "evaluation and a reassessment of my needs." The doctors ran whatever tests that were available in those days, all of which simply confirmed what we already knew: I have organic brain damage that significantly limits my intellectual capacity. I throw tantrums that sometimes escalate into seizures when I'm really angry. I eat well. And I will never be able to take care of myself. What I need is a warm, loving, protective environment with enough structure to help me get through the day.

Believe it or not, I stayed in that hospital for over a year. The doctors and nurses were all very nice to me. There was always plenty to eat. But it was very confusing because I wasn't sick. We Catholics used to have this concept of limbo, which supposedly was where babies go if they happen to die before being baptized. Baptism is the only ticket to heaven, you see. But since babies haven't done anything to warrant sending them to that other place where it's so hot all the time, God created a special spot for them that is the next best thing to heaven.

But I *was* baptized and *wasn't* dead, so why did I get stuck in my version of limbo?

The answer: Mom was stalling for time. She didn't know what else to do with me and didn't want me to wind up wasting away on a back ward.

The hospital finally had to take Mom and Fred to court to force them to come and get me. In yet another ironic twist to my story—plenty more lie ahead—the juvenile court judge who handed down the decision was none other than Chris's future father-in-law.

I'm telling you again, you can't make this stuff up.

CATHOLICS ALSO BELIEVE in guardian angels, with what happened next making it impossible to doubt *their* existence. Someone put Mom in touch with a Mennonite family that she was told might be willing to foster a disabled teenager. Mom called the Yoders and found out they had seven children, one of whom was even developmentally disabled like me. Rebecca was two years younger and couldn't talk either. They owned a small farm in the Shenandoah Valley and said to Mom they sure could use the extra income from the survivor benefits that I had begun receiving after Daddy died.

It was a win across the board. Mom had found me a good home and could stop feeling like a bad mother, at least temporarily. I would be part of a sprawling family already familiar with the nuances of caring for me. And Henry and Ruth could stop worrying about paying their mortgage on time because the monthly checks I received from the government would be enough to cover it.

So Mom and Fred picked me up from the hospital in Fred's big Buick and drove me three hours south to the Yoder's place just outside Waynesboro, Virginia. I've always loved riding in the car so much that it doesn't matter to me where we're going. But the Shenandoah Valley happens to be one of the most beautiful places on earth.

The whole family came out to greet us. They were dressed so differently! The boys wore button-down shirts and straw hats like their father, and Ruth and the girls had on bonnets and long skirts. Everybody looked so healthy and happy.

Not realizing this was another one-way trip, I felt more confused than ever when Mom said goodbye and drove off with Fred. Why had she looked almost as sad as she did after Daddy died?

I wonder if it ever occurred to Mom how often history repeats itself, especially within families. Here she was dropping me off on a farm to be taken care of by strangers just like her mother and father had once done with her.

But I loved it immediately. We had cows, and pigs, and chickens, and a dog that didn't kill cats—or chickens either. Actually, it was a lot like when Daddy was alive. Ruth stayed home and took care of the house and the garden, Rebecca and me, and the younger kids. The older ones rode the bus to school. Henry went to work in the barn or out in the fields, and he was always at the head of the table for meals. Ruth was a great cook, and our food was fresh and delicious.

Plus no one drank a drop.

To top it all off, there was never any turmoil. Ruth and Henry were both calm, patient people, all about raising children. Breakfast, lunch, and dinner were always at the same time, and we went to church as a family every Sunday. My new brothers and sisters all called me Susie, which I very much liked.

Ruth treated me as one of her own and gradually taught me to do the kinds of chores that Rebecca did to help out. I learned how to set a proper table: the napkin and fork on the left side of the plate, the spoon and knife on the right, with the knife closest to the plate. I could clear and wipe the table after we had finished eating, too, and after a while I was even able to carry out the slop bucket and dump it on the ground for the pigs. It felt so satisfying to be a contributing member of a household.

One day on the farm flowed seamlessly into the next. The routines never changed. Everyone knew their place in the order of things and was content to be in that place. As for me, I woke up each morning raring to go. I hardly ever got sick, and tantrums and seizures became a thing of the past.

Life was good again. Everything made sense.

JFK'S YOUNGER SISTER Eunice devoted most of her

life to helping developmentally disabled children. One of the things she did every summer, with her husband Sargent Shriver's help, was to turn their suburban Maryland estate into a camp for fifty or so developmentally disabled and autistic kids. Approximately half of the campers came on a bus from the Maryland State Hospital. It was just like a normal summer camp, with horses to ride, a pond for canoeing, and a big swimming pool. Except that the kids weren't normal at all, and they each had their own counselor.

The Shrivers recruited the counselors by sending invitations to all the private high schools in the area. In the summer of '70, Chris, probably missing his connection with me, volunteered to be one of them. So did my sister-in-law-to-be Betsy, whose father had ordered Mom and Fred to reclaim me from the hospital.

The young members of the Kennedy clan were counselors, too. Chris and Betsy worked side by side with them, and Betsy even went on a few dates with the son of Peter Lawford, the famous actor married to one of JFK's other sisters. Also named Chris, he started taking Betsy out in his new red convertible. My Chris, who already had his eye on her, was insanely jealous.

Just this year, by the way, Eunice received a posthumous ESPY award because of the way Camp Shriver grew into the Special Olympics. Which at this point is a global movement of over four and a half million developmentally disabled athletes. She believed that when we're given the same experiences and opportunities as everyone else, we can accomplish far more than anyone ever thought possible. Amen to that, too.

Meanwhile, my Chris had no idea how much JFK's legacy was about to affect my life.

When Camp Shriver was over for the summer, my Chris finally decided to ask Betsy out. Lucky for him, by then she had concluded that the other Chris was a little too full of himself. Although it was Betsy who made the first move. One morning she showed up at our house with a coffee can full of the same homemade, chocolate chip cookies my Chris had praised to the skies at the end-of-camp party. It turned out she only lived a mile away, so he invited her to a dance at the parish teen center.

They went to visit Betsy's camper for their second date. A nine-year-old boy with Down syndrome, Stein was one of the back ward kids. He was playing in the day room with a group of five or six others when Chris and Betsy arrived. The boys surrounded them like a pack of hungry wolves the moment their visitors walked through the doors—talk about desperate for attention. One of them begged Chris to let him wear his watch, and Chris had one helluva time getting it back again when it was time to say goodbye to Stein.

All the boys were much too skinny, as though they were underfed as well. And their skin was pasty, suggesting that they didn't see the out-of-doors very often.

Betsy burst into tears as soon as she got back in Chris's car. She and Chris had heard the terrible stories about the back wards, but experiencing one firsthand was another thing altogether.

They've been spending a lot of time together ever since.

FRED NEVER RECOVERED from his failed condo project and eventually decided to pull up stakes and relocate to the northernmost county in Maryland, where he had heard that there would be more development opportunities. Mom kept the house on 42nd St. and her job at NIH for the time being, and she and Fred saw each other on weekends. But the separation was another stress on an already strained relationship. So Mom reluctantly quit her job a few months later, in order for her and Sam to move up to be with Fred.

John was married by then. He and his wife Kathy had bought a ramshackle farmhouse on the Eastern Shore of Maryland, where John began his life as a country-rock musician. John and Kathy had gone to Woodstock together in '69 and spent a week dancing in the mud with a half-million other hippies.

John would never be the same after that. To help pay the mortgage when his band wasn't getting enough gigs, he started making marijuana bongs out of Plexiglass and selling them in beach towns up and down the Shore. They were so popular that he even trademarked the name—TokeMaster! But when the state banned pot paraphernalia, John sold the design and the trademark to a guy who cleverly changed the name to TobaccoMaster to skirt the new law. You can still buy one today, fifty years later, and John's brilliant design hasn't changed one iota.

About to graduate from high school, Chris stayed on alone at 42nd St. through the following summer. As soon as school was out, he got a job working construction and then went off to a college in southern Virginia in the Fall. He would never move back in with Mom, Fred, and Sam either.

Mom, ever the survivor, managed to get a job as the secretary for the warden of Cecil County's new jail for women. Just like at NIH, she quickly became her boss's right hand and played a big role in turning the jail into a model facility.

Samantha entered the second grade in a rural K-8 school run by a small order of French nuns. She was very happy there and always at the top of her class.

Fred went on being Fred.

FOUR

As my days with the Yoders turned into years, the arrangement was obviously becoming permanent. Ruth and Henry felt like a second mom and dad, and Rebecca like a sister. I was delighted with things just the way they were.

So sure enough, one day Ruth and Henry called Mom and Fred to say that, if it was okay with them, they would like to adopt me. The year was 1976.

Mom knew it was for the best. She said yes almost immediately, but there was still a pang of reluctance. The thought of officially giving me up, even though I was by then a young woman, stirred her guilt over having let me go before. I had been born from her flesh. I was her first daughter. And Chris and I were a deep connection to Daddy and a time when everything in her life had made sense, too. Maybe the only time.

Fred? He didn't think twice.

In the end, they all agreed to set the court date three months in the future to give Mom time to be totally sure she was okay with the idea.

Then my guardian angel decided to take a little nap. Or

I guess Fred wasn't the only one whose luck had a lousy habit of going south just when things were getting good. As the court date approached, Ruth discovered she was pregnant again. At forty-two she was caught completely off guard. She and Henry went over and over the situation, only to keep reaching the same sober conclusion: Nine kids, including a newborn baby and two disabled daughters, would simply be too much for Ruth to manage. They were going to have to call off the adoption and give me back to Mom and Fred.

There I was only weeks away from becoming Susan Yoder. You could say it had been my one shot at marriage, in my case to a whole family. Just what does that expression mean, "It wasn't meant to be?"

Susan Mercogliano was 22 and homeless once again.

MOM WAS STAGGERED. She had no clue where to turn for help with my predicament, and the clock was ticking fast.

Little did Mom know that she had already solved the problem simply by moving to Cecil County. Maryland had answered JFK's mandate two years earlier by opening a very community-based ICF for developmentally disabled children and adults on the Eastern Shore. Better still, it was free to state residents, which technically I now was.

My angel woke up just in time to somehow help Mom find out about Holly Center. When Mom called, the director told her that the center was not yet filled to capacity and that I could move in right away.

So, eight years later, back came Mom and Fred. This

time Fred was driving a big, white Lincoln Continental, a trophy left over from a score he'd made while I was with the Yoders. Everyone came out to the car to say goodbye. Ruth was crying as she hugged me, and Henry looked sad, too. Mom looked even sadder.

Once again, it was all very confusing. Why was I leaving this place that I loved so much? And where was I going?

The answer was straight to Holly Center, a five-hour drive heading north and then east. I don't think Mom or Fred said a word the entire time, while I stared silently out the window watching the world rush by.

Mom was told to bring me to cottage 300. Fred carried in my belongings and then retreated to the car to wait for her.

After Mom had a long talk with the head of the cottage, they walked me down the corridor to my room. It was freshly painted, and all the furnishings were still like new. Mom sat quietly with me for a while, and then she started crying just like Ruth had earlier. Mom was not a big crier—nor am I for that matter. It was the first time I ever remembered seeing her in tears.

Mom told me how much she loved me and that she would come back to visit soon. But the moment she was gone, my all-too-familiar confusion exploded into rage. So many huge changes all at once had left me completely overwhelmed.

Suddenly, just like in the old days, I was yelling and hitting myself in the head as hard as I could with my fist. The nurse and an aide rushed in to try to calm me down, but it was too late. The tantrum had already mushroomed into a full-blown seizure. Then all my fuses blew, and I blacked out.

I would never know that Mom was watching me the whole time through the window in my door.

TO SAY THAT Holly Center is community-based is the literal truth—as opposed to privatized group homes, which call themselves "community-based" even though most of them aren't. But here I go fast-forwarding again.

Holly Center was conceived and birthed entirely by people here in Wicomico County. It all began in early 1967 when the Wicomico Association for Retarded Citizens decided to conduct a comprehensive, county-wide survey of the support needs of families with developmentally disabled children and adults. WARC then held a bunch of chicken barbecues to raise money for the printing and distribution of 500 copies of the resulting document.

The survey demonstrated an urgent need for a facility on the Eastern Shore that could provide housing, medical care, and life and job training. So next, WARC organized a big letter-writing campaign aimed at informing state and county officials about the survey results. Pretty soon the media picked up the story, and within a year the County Council voted to create a special commission to plan the center and lobby the state to pay for it.

It didn't take long for the state legislature to approve the funding. Salisbury was chosen as the center's location because of its greater concentration of people in need of services, as well as a plentiful supply of community resources to help support the center moving forward.

It was even WARC and a couple of other local citizen groups that procured the site for the center. Somehow they managed to convince the County Council to sell a seventy-five-acre parcel of land on the eastern edge of the city to the state for the grand total of ten bucks.

The state senator who had lobbied strongly for a Salisbury location, Mary Nock, was given the honor of naming the center. She chose "Holly" because it's such a hardy, beautiful tree that can grow just about anywhere. Amen and amen.

Holly Center welcomed its first residents in January of '75. They were escapees from the Rosewood Hospital Center, a state hospital built just outside Baltimore in 1888—originally known as the Asylum and Training School for the Feeble-Minded.

That's right folks; you cannot make this stuff up.

HOLLY CENTER WAS built to accommodate 225 people, and what I'm about to describe is the center as it remained until the late 1980s. I'll explain how and why things began to change as the story unfolds.

There were nine cottages in the beginning, with residents grouped according to age and level of need. Some of us live here year-round and some come for respite care when their families need a break. Or some stay just long enough to learn the necessary skills for living in smaller group homes, or even out on your own like Turk. I'll tell you more about him later, too. There's even a children's school, which I sure wish had been around when I was a kid.

The center's mission is the same as that of Eunice Shriver and the Special Olympics. They provide us with whatever types of support we need to maximize our potential and make life on the inside as similar as possible to life on the outside.

No one wastes away here. We have a gym where those of us who are physically able can engage in all kinds of games and sports. And then the gym converts into an auditorium for special events like plays, concerts, dances, and a church service on Sundays. We have a big indoor swimming pool, too, which they keep extra warm for therapeutic purposes. There's even a canteen with a soda fountain, where we can hold smaller parties or just hang out with our families when they come to visit. Plus there's my favorite place of all—the thrift shop!

We celebrate all the major holidays together, and the calendar is full of other social events as well. One of the amazing things about Holly Center is how connected we are to the Salisbury area. Thousands of people come to our Spring Festival every year, when we set up booths to sell crafts and baked goods. There are bands playing, too, and clowns, marionettes, and pony rides for the kids. It's a really fun time and raises a lot of money for the Holly Foundation, which uses the funds for things like trips and birthday and holiday gifts for those of us without much family involvement.

The Christmas Bazaar is very popular, too. Vendors from all over the Eastern Shore bring their holiday wares to sell. Then there's Antique Weekend in the Fall, which works the same way, along with the Black Heritage Fair and the

Carnival of Food and Culture. All the events are fundraisers for the foundation, as are the bikeathon and the swimathon that also take place on campus.

One of the reasons there's always so much going on here is that more than 600 individuals and 50 different groups volunteer their time to help the center with everything they're trying to do for us. It's an incredible show of community support, and there isn't much they haven't thought of. We even have our own form of Big Brother Big Sister program that provides those of us who need it with a one-on-one relationship with an outside sponsor. There's also a foster grandparent program for our young people.

And it isn't just the community coming to us; we get out into the community all the time. There are buses and vans for field trips to all sorts of interesting places. We patronize theaters and restaurants, and shop at real stores at the mall. We attend concerts at the local colleges. We visit area museums and galleries. We go out to ball games and up to Baltimore to root for our guys in the Special Olympics. And every June we hang out downtown at the Salisbury Festival, unless the weather is too hot, and sometimes there are even overnights in places like Ocean City. Plus every summer there's a picnic for the whole center at Shad Landing State Park. Volunteers bring their signature dishes, and the food is amazing.

Another important thing a group of volunteers and staff does is to make presentations in the local schools about people with disabilities. One of the main reasons why society hid us away on those back wards for so many generations was that there has always been a big stigma attached to physical and mental anomalies. So now the idea is to teach kids that all of us struggle against obstacles in life. The obstacles just look different depending on the abilities we're born with, or if illnesses or accidents take some of our abilities away.

The schools then reciprocate by sending over junior volunteers to provide us with companionship. What better way for children to learn that our basic needs are the same as everyone else's?

Even the surroundings are beautiful here. In the early days, we were ringed by huge fields of corn and soybeans destined for Frank Perdue's chickens. Some of that land has since sprouted houses instead, but there's still a rural feel because the center owns so much undeveloped acreage. And our campus keeps getting prettier and more peaceful as the trees, which were only saplings when I moved in, continue to grow taller and broader. There are also screened-in gazebos for picnics, and many years ago volunteers put in a wonderful perennial flower and herb garden for us, too.

It's no wonder that the results of the annual Family/Advocate Satisfaction Survey hover between 98 and 100%.

I WOKE UP THE next morning completely out of sorts. I had rebounded okay, but it was so strange being back in an institutional setting after all those wonderful years on the farm. Once again there were no fathers, no horses, no creeks, no dogs. As for mothers, Mom was so wracked with guilt after witnessing my seizure that she wouldn't return until years later.

Sorry, I'm skipping forward again.

I nevertheless had an immediately good feeling about this place. The staff always seemed to be smiling, and everyone was extremely nice to me. It was a genuine, affectionate nice, too, not the superficial, professional type that I have encountered elsewhere.

Plus I think everyone finds comfort in being surrounded by people who are more or less like themselves. Not that just as much diversity doesn't exist among us at Holly Center as within the rest of humanity, but you know what I mean.

We are glaringly unlike people on the outside, and at the same time we're also quite different from each other. There's an even mix of men and women, some with white skin, some light brown, and some dark. Some are young adults like me when I first arrived and some are much older like I am now. Some of us are verbal, but many are not. Some of us can walk, while others need wheelchairs to get around. A few can't see; a few can't hear.

What a cast of characters we were in cottage 300 the year I moved in, each with such a unique personality. Tommy, even though chair-bound and nonverbal, was our ambassador. He was right there to greet visitors when they arrived. His entire face crinkled when he smiled, and he welcomed everyone with a handshake, or better still a little innocent hand-holding. Tommy was a big hugger as well—and still is today. He and I have grown old here together.

I already told you a little about Cindy. She had a sweet, childlike face and spoke in a faint whisper that made her difficult to hear. She always kept her eyes closed, too, as though she were talking in her sleep even though she was wide awake. We liked to sit next to each on the couch in the foyer, which was another reason why it was so easy to sneak her things into my purse. After several years with us in 300, Cindy moved to a nice group home that opened up closer to her parents. That way they could spend even more time together.

Then there was Vanessa, who was highly verbal. She befriended me even though I couldn't talk, and she would talk to me even though I never answered back. Probably the thing I appreciated most about her was that she was willful and sneaky like me. The staff was always scolding her for doing things she wasn't supposed to, but don't think that stopped her even for a second. She knew just what to say to keep anyone from getting too mad at her.

Jeanette was another one with a glint in her eye. Tall and slender with an imposing glare, she cussed like a Marine when things didn't go her way. Name-dropping was her go-to strategy for getting around the rules: "Yesterday Connie told me it's okay for me to go to the canteen whenever I want."

Me? I was the inscrutable one, always present—I mentioned how good I am at that—and always taking it all in. I understood whatever the staff was saying to me and had no trouble following directions at work. As a matter of fact, I was one of my boss's favorites because my work was so steady, and I rarely missed a day. But I was like a Trappist monk with his vow of silence. Or a happy twelve-month-old who looks at you with those alert, knowing eyes that leave you wondering what she would have to say if only she could.

Talk to anyone who's ever spent much time around me and they'll tell you I'm way more intelligent than appears at first glance. Just ask Scottie, who's been on the staff for 39 years. One night I picked out the wrong pajamas while she was helping me shower and get ready for bed. "The tops and the bottoms don't match," she told me. "Go back and switch one of them." And I did precisely that.

While Tommy and Vanessa are friendly and outgoing, I'm not in the least. It's not that I'm antisocial. I like plenty of people, especially little children. But I prefer to keep my own counsel, to pick and choose when to let in others.

Maybe the right word is cautious. When you've been hurt as many times as I have, wouldn't you think twice before you decide it's safe to get close?

FIVE

One of the things I valued most about living with the Yoders was being useful. I understand why Mom had needed her daily soap opera fix—that's what housewives did back then. But I've never been one to sit around in front of a television because it's so darn boring. Chris loves to quote the famous architect Frank Lloyd Wright on this score: "TV is chewing gum for the eyes." Wright wasn't kidding.

So it was like I had died and gone to heaven when Holly Center started sending me to Somerset for job training. Add in the half-hour bus ride down sleepy Route 413 and back, and I really was in heaven.

Somerset is what they used to call a "sheltered workshop." Altogether there were about 70 of us and ten staff, who very patiently taught us how to do the simple jobs that local businesses were contracting out to us. I already mentioned packaging vending machine trinkets. We also did things like stick labels on jars, and stuff envelopes for bulk mailings. Then one time we were even hired to assemble doormats, the kind made out of horizontal strips of hard rubber that have a space between them and are held together by a wire frame.

The material for the mats came in different colors, and so on different days we got to make them in different patterns. Learning a new pattern was a bit tricky at first, but it was a cinch once you caught on. I thought the mats came out really nice. After about a year, unfortunately, the company stopped producing the mats because they couldn't get the right kind of rubber anymore.

Sheltered workshops became controversial because some people decided the workshops were a way of segregating developmentally disabled people from the rest of society. Those naysayers also thought businesses were getting away with paying us less than we're worth just because we're disabled, meaning the workshops were a form of exploitation, too. So there's been a big push all around the country to close them and encourage employers to integrate us into mainstream workplaces instead.

It's hard to argue against things like inclusion and equality, but I'm getting confused again—and ahead of myself as usual. What's going to happen to people like me who need more support than will be available out in the marketplace?

It goes without saying that people who are able enough should have the same opportunities as everyone else. Like Turk, whom I'll tell you more about now. His full name is Turkmenogluen Deniz, so you can see why people simply call him Turk. His father was once a prominent doctor on the Eastern Shore, but when Turk was four, the dad put him in a residential school for developmentally disabled kids and disappeared back to his native Turkey.

I don't know whether Turk aged out of the school or his

father quit paying the tuition like Fred did with me. Either way, Turk found himself on the back ward of the Rosewood State Hospital at the ripe old age of 10—never to be seen again if not for Holly Center. Which would've been criminal because Turk wasn't all that disabled to begin with.

Thankfully Holly Center opened its doors five years later, with Turk as one of our first residents along with the other people from Rosewood that I mentioned. The staff picked up on Turk's intelligence right away. They began working with him on housekeeping and kitchen cleaning skills and also helped him learn how to cook for himself and manage his own money so that he would be able to live independently.

Pretty soon Turk was working part-time at a local hotel. Then right after Turk turned twenty-one, his case manager helped him land a full-time janitor's position at a nursing home in nearby Easton. Steve also helped Turk find an apartment not far from the job, where he has been living on his own ever since. He still gets weekly check-ins from a support person to make sure he's getting along okay.

Obviously, Turk didn't belong at Somerset with me. But what I'm especially concerned about—not that I'll be around for it to matter—is that profoundly disabled people who can't handle *un*sheltered work are going to wind up with nothing else to do besides squandering their time in front of the boob tube in a day room somewhere.

That's not right either. It means that once again society's most vulnerable members won't have access to the help they need to lead the fullest lives possible.

The situation is as tangled up as a ball of yarn the cat got into. It involves economic issues like funding and political ones like the extent to which the government should involve itself in people's lives. Let's just leave it that I have never felt segregated or exploited at Somerset; in fact, I loved working there so much that on the days when some kind of appointment interfered, they had to bamboozle me to keep me from throwing a fit. They would do things like drive me to the doctor's office in one of our big buses so that at least it *felt* like I was going to work. Which did the trick every time.

I'll come back to this thread in a minute when the continued existence of Holly Center starts coming into question.

WHEN I MOVED here in '77, John didn't live on the Eastern Shore anymore. He was likewise in an institution, only his wasn't quite as community-based as mine. Haha. John's bong business, you see, had drawn the attention of the local authorities, and one day in 1974 they set up a sting operation to entrap him. A deputy sheriff posing as a friend of one of John's "friends" busted John as soon as John sold him a small amount of pot to go along with a TokeMaster— which by itself was still legal.

Up for reelection that year, the district attorney in Cambridge did his best to throw the book at John, who ended up being sentenced to three years in a state penitentiary in western Maryland. His relationship with Kathy had already begun to fray around the edges, and then it completely unraveled while he was away. This would spell the end of the

Eastern Shore for him.

Mom continued helping the warden run their non-community-based institution in Elkton, a job she thoroughly enjoyed. Fred was up to his usual shenanigans, and Sam started attending a Catholic high school in Bel Air.

Chris and Betsy had both dropped out of college after their freshman year—Mom was crushed when Chris informed her of his decision—and then in the Fall of '73 they moved up to Albany, NY to volunteer at an inner-city free school that Chris had read about in a book while he was studying education at Washington and Lee. Neither had the hippie gene like John. The reason they quit school, in addition to wanting to live together, was to find a way to change the world right then and there. They settled on working with kids who needed help the most.

I HADN'T SEEN Chris since going to live with the Yoders, and now he was 400 miles away. But that wasn't the only thing keeping him from visiting me until I had already been here a couple of years. Mom always kept him informed about my whereabouts, so he knew I had moved to Holly Center after the Yoders. She had told him what a nice place it is, but I don't think he entirely trusted her. He was afraid she might be airbrushing the picture because he sensed how much guilt she was carrying over having given me up.

Nor did it help that the day Chris and Betsy had spent on the back ward with those boys was still fresh in his mind. He was worried he might find me in similar straits. So it took some pretty persistent encouragement from Betsy before he finally decided to take the plunge and drive down to see me.

I think he was also concerned that I might not recognize him anymore because it had been so long. We were young teenagers the last time we saw each other, and now we were full-blown adults. But you know how time seems to stand still when you haven't seen someone you're close to for a long stretch. And you also know how much I live in the moment, and so of course I knew it was Chris when he finally walked through the front door, long ponytail and all.

They had told him to come on a Saturday to keep me from missing my shift at Somerset, and there I was chilling with Cindy in the foyer the morning he arrived. He had spent the night before in DC with Betsy's mom and dad— my old friend Judge Ketcham. Tommy was out there with us, too. He wheeled right over to help put Chris at ease, and the worry lines on Chris's face faded as soon as Tommy took hold of his hand and then pulled him down for a hug.

Chris got to meet all the cottage staff who were working that day. Their warm friendliness reassured him even more. Since he's a big walker like me, pretty soon we were wandering all over the campus together. He was blown away by the beauty. Scottie had told him the canteen was always open and to please help ourselves, so we stopped in on our way back to the cottage. My weakness for Pepsi caused me to guzzle way too much, while we also feasted on a big jar of peanut butter crackers.

What was there to possibly worry about?

When the time came for Chris to leave, he grew visibly

sad. He was trying his best to hide it, but I could tell he was crying on the inside. It wasn't guilt he was wrestling with like Mom. He recognized how happy I am here and how I'm exactly where I need to be. But later on when he and Betsy began to visit me regularly, he would tell her as they drove away that he felt like he was leaving a piece of himself behind.

This is how they say twins feel when they're separated.

LIFE AT HOLLY Center became a lot like life with the Yoders. It even smelled the same every time the farmer next door spread manure on his fields! The only difference, other than there being more of them, was that my new "siblings" were all biologically unrelated. But a big, unorthodox family we were nonetheless. Days merged into weeks, weeks into months, and my unchanging routine remained a huge comfort. I spent weekdays hard at work at Somerset, and on weekends we went out and did all the interesting things I talked about earlier.

One time they even took us to the race track to see the trotters. I like horses best of all, so who cares if we never placed any bets? I was happy just to sit there all afternoon watching those gorgeous animals run by, pulling their sulkies and drivers behind them.

Another time when we went to the movies to see *The Lone Ranger,* I brought along one of my stuffed ponies. I galloped her across my lap right in stride with the horses on the screen during the chase scenes.

Speaking of stuffed animals, every so often we used to

hit up the big flea market out on Route 13. One day we happened upon a card table covered with second-hand teddy bears, dogs, unicorns, and other assorted creatures. The woman who was selling them said I could have as many as I wanted for free, even though I had my own money with me. Recognizing that my handbag was already bursting at the seams, she even—oh so naively—gave me a big shopping bag to put them in. I'm glad Sam and Chris weren't there to warn her. In two blinks of an eye, I had cleared off the lot.

There's always something fun to do in and around Salisbury, but my hands-down favorite activity is an annual one that takes place right here at the center. Every December the Perdue chicken people, who have a large presence here on the Shore, send over a convoy of 18-wheelers to take everyone for a joyride on the highway. The drivers and their families decorate their rigs like Christmas trees, and whoever does the best job gets a prize. One year the winner was a vegetable oil tanker wrapped in red and white stripes like a giant candy cane.

I'll never forget the first time. Since it wasn't a particularly cold morning, we bundled up and waited out in front of the gym for the trucks to arrive. What a sight to behold when they started turning in off of Snow Hill Rd., air horns blaring. There had to have been at least fifty, some from as far away as North Carolina, and there was barely enough room for them in the parking lot. Santa and one of his elves made an appearance, too, along with a whole crowd of people who came just to watch. And one of the local television stations sent a camera crew and reporter. It was a real circus.

A bunch of great big Salisbury University football players also showed up to hoist us up into the cabs. Before you knew it, they had somehow managed to get us all buckled in next to our drivers. Mine was wearing a Santa hat and grinning from ear to ear. So was I once he eased that bad boy into gear, and we rumbled back out onto Snow Hill. It was way more exciting than the bus because you can see so much more when you're sitting up in the front seat eight feet above the pavement!

As soon as we were cruising on the Salisbury bypass, Lonnie picked up his CB radio mic. "Breaker one-nine, this is Chicken Man here. I got Miss Sue-Sue next to me, and she looks like she's havin' a real nice time."

"Copy that, Chicken Man. This is Big John right back at ya. Tommy's my co-pilot, and he ain't stopped smilin' yet."

Wouldn't you know the news crew had climbed in behind Tommy and was capturing his ecstasy on camera? It was extremely funny watching him later on the six o'clock news doing his best version of the Cheshire Cat. He's so scrunched up all the time that he really had to crane his neck to look out of the window.

After everyone had returned, the drivers, their families, and all the volunteers joined us back at the gym for a big Christmas party.

Mind you, Santa always appears again later in the month to hand out presents, but this is my sweetest day of the year. It isn't just that I love going for rides so much, but also because the event was inspired by a famous Red Sovine song about a boy with a story a bit like mine.

The boy in the song is "crippled and can't walk," and his daddy was a trucker who the month before had jackknifed and died on the Interstate in the middle of a blizzard. After that, the boy's mom gets a job to support them and has to leave him alone at home with only his daddy's CB radio to keep him company.

His mom tells him just to listen in and not disturb guys while they're driving, but one day he's so lonely that he breaks in anyway and asks if someone out there is willing to talk to a ten-year-old. "Teddy Bear" is his handle, and he gets an immediate response from a long-distance hauler like his father. Teddy Bear proceeds to tell him his story, adding that he wishes he could ride in a big rig one day because his daddy had promised to take his mom and him on the road that coming summer.

As the trucker is signing off, he asks Teddy Bear his address but doesn't reveal why. Then, as the song goes, the driver makes a U-turn and heads straight to Jackson Street, 229. There's already a line of 18-wheelers in front of Teddy Bear's house three blocks long when he arrives. That's because all the other truckers in the area had been listening in, and they wanted to make Teddy Bear's day, too. One by one they take him out for a spin, and his mom returns home from work just as he's coming in from his last ride.

Every trucker listens to country music, so it was Red's song that inspired the guys from Perdue to bring what they call "Operation Teddy Bear" to Holly Center every Christmas. It's now in its thirty-something-eth year.

So yeah, life was good again. Real good.

BUT THEN THE State of Maryland started putting pressure on Holly Center to transfer as many of us as possible into privately-run group homes. They said it was part of the same push for more community inclusion and less restrictive care that was causing the closure of sheltered workshops.

Mom received a letter from the director of the center explaining the new policy and asking her to please consider several of what the director considered to be excellent group home options for me. But the state would not, the letter concluded, force me to leave Holly Center. If Mom still wanted me here after checking out the alternatives, then so be it.

Mom and Fred went to visit the first place on the list and quickly decided they'd seen enough. Although the house was certainly homier than Holly Center and sat on a nice residential street, with all 12 residents appearing to be well cared for, everyone was functioning at a much higher level than me. The staff also seemed much less experienced than my caregivers here, which left too many question marks. What if I had a seizure or got really sick? What would happen as I got older, and my needs began to increase? What if we tried it, and things didn't work out?

The operator of the home assured Mom that they would always be able to provide me with adequate care. And then came the kicker: "Don't you want Susan to have the chance to live in a home setting again, Mrs. Shulley?"

Mom answered that she wanted time to think it over and consult with the rest of the family. When she called John, Chris, and Sam and described the situation, all three agreed that the move was simply too risky. Besides, Holly Center is a wonderful place, and Susan feels perfectly at home *there.*

So Mom called our director and said absolutely not. Holly Center is where my daughter belongs. End of discussion.

Ever the suspicious type, Chris decided to take a closer look at why the state was suddenly trying to get us all to leave Holly Center. His take was that the center was a creature of the cooperative spirit of the '60s and '70s when there was a widespread belief that people can come together at the grassroots level and change things for the better. It was the same spirit that had gotten the school going in Albany where he and Betsy had gone to teach. It even took root in a conservative backwater like the Eastern Shore and inspired the people who created Holly Center. After that it fed all the wonderful community support we've been receiving ever since.

It was a time when it *was* seen as the government's responsibility to help improve people's lives, especially those in the greatest need. JFK's New Frontier was followed by LBJ's Great Society and the War on Poverty, and those policies led to the funding of all kinds of government programs aimed at solving social problems. The spirit was so strong that it even survived the next two Republican presidents.

But then, according to Chris, there was a huge swing of the pendulum when Ronald Reagan got elected in 1980. "Government" suddenly became a dirty word. It's too big, said the conservatives. It's wasteful. It intrudes on people's lives. Worse still, it fosters dependency. In America, people are supposed to pull themselves up by their own bootstraps.

And their unspoken bottom line: it's bad for business.

After his massive tax cuts for big corporations and the rich quickly tripled the national debt, Reagan and his cohorts started selling the country on the idea that the answer to the crisis they'd just created was to take public entities like utilities, hospitals, nursing homes, schools, and prisons and put them in private hands. They preached the gospel that competition and corporate know-how will get things done more efficiently.

Support services for the developmentally disabled were some of the first to be privatized. Corporations that were allegedly nonprofit, and an increasing number of for-profit ones, took full advantage of the movement to liberate us from inhuman institutions like Willowbrook. They opened up chains of small, privately operated group homes and established a national organization called the ARC— which stood for the Association for Retarded Children until "retarded" became a politically incorrect term—to lobby for the closing of *all* state-run facilities. Even the good ICFs like Holly Center.

In the end they did a very convincing job of turning "institution" into a dirty word, too.

The conservatives got their way, Chris says, just like they usually do. Our care was no longer a public service. Now it was a private industry. The group homes were still funded by tax dollars, but the owners' claim that they could do it for less was music to every politician's ears. No one seemed concerned that the way they would do it more cheaply would be by hiring staff with less training and experience and paying them a fraction of what a staff person gets here, and by providing care that isn't nearly as comprehensive as the kind we receive.

Chris has a good friend in Albany who works for the state agency overseeing group homes. She told him that high staff turnover due to low pay is a huge problem and that many group homes aren't meeting all the care needs of highly disabled people like me. But whenever she tries to alert her bosses, her words fall on deaf ears because the state is determined to cut costs any way it can.

Just like the sheltered workshop issue that I brought up earlier, it's complicated. There's no question that they *should* stop hiding us away and help us lead lives that are as normal as possible. And yes, group homes often are situated in real neighborhoods. The good ones *are* more home-like than Holly Center. So for people less disabled than me, group homes make sense. Or if people like Turk can live independently with the help of a social worker, all the better. But what about the rest of us?

When Chris talked to Hugo Dwyer, the head of a national organization that advocates for the developmentally and intellectually disabled called Voice of Reason, he told Chris there are several areas of concern. One is that the government has never been willing to allocate enough money to address the needs of all disabled people. Even though JFK was able to convince Congress to pass his bill to fund better care and education for many of us, the amount he managed to secure was a drop in the bucket. And the situation has been the same ever since. If anything, it's only gotten worse.

Another problem is that the focus always seems to be on higher-functioning individuals who appear more normal than me. For some reason it's much harder for policymakers to put themselves in my shoes and identify with my extreme vulnerability.

The other problem is they never built enough Holly Centers. We remained a showcase facility, meaning too few people have had a chance to see that not all institutions are bad. As a result, the politicians deciding our fate don't realize how ICFs like Holly Center will always be the best option for individuals with a high degree of need.

We'll talk more about this when I get to my cottage mate Ginger.

LUCKY FOR ME, many of the other Holly Center families felt the same way mine did. Some of us began transitioning out into group homes, but there was enough pushback against the idea to force the state to keep the center open, at least for the time being.

They still kept the heat on, however. Every year, for example, the team responsible for my well-being meets with me and Mom—and then Sam and Chris after Mom was gone—to go over my care with a fine-tooth comb. And from that point on, each annual review concludes with the team leader asking them if they would be willing to consider moving me to a group home. And every year they repeat, "NO!"

Here I should finally mention something good about

Fred. On several occasions during this period, he phoned the director of Holly Center and threatened to go all the way up to the governor if they didn't stop talking about shutting down the center. After Fred was out of the picture, too, and the talk grew even louder, Sam and Chris followed suit by writing strongly worded letters to the state agency that funds the center.

But I'm afraid I'm getting ahead of myself—*again*.

SIX

There's another nice thing to say about Fred: After John had served half his jail term, Fred used his real estate connections to arrange a meeting with the governor's office. Every year, the governor issues a handful of Christmas pardons, and somehow Fred managed to get John's name on the list. Then Fred helped John find work in a sawmill in North Carolina so that he could get back on his feet again. It wasn't exactly a bandleader's cup of tea, but jobs are hard to come by when you're an ex-convict.

Meanwhile, life was also good for Mom and Fred. Mom loved her job at the jail and the beautiful house they had found, which sat on a cliff overlooking the upper reaches of the Chesapeake Bay. Fred had successfully rebuilt his business. Samantha was doing well in school and in the process of becoming an award-winning flute player. And I had stopped being a source of concern.

This was the period when Mom got seriously into writing. Serving on the jury in a long, drawn-out murder trial full of twists and turns inspired her to take a shot at writing a murder mystery of her own. She called the novel

Caprice, and it was good enough for a local literary agent to try to find a publisher.

The fact that there were never any takers didn't discourage Mom in the least. She went on to write another book called *A Woman's Guide to Watching Football,* and this one did get consideration because it was right when football was becoming popular on television. A lifelong fan of the Washington Redskins, Mom knew her stuff. But no one picked up that manuscript either.

Around the same time, Fred pulled off the kind of coup developers dream about. After hearing through the grapevine that they were going to put in a new exit on I-95 just north of where he and Mom had settled, he quietly worked out a deal with the farmer who owned the adjacent land. Fred simultaneously negotiated with gas stations and fast-food joints interested in buying subdivided pieces of the property so that they could do business there, and then he somehow managed to close on all the deals on the same day. Which meant that in the end, it was Burger King and McDonald's paying the farmer, not Fred. Plus there was a whole lot left over for him.

Fred Shulley was no dummy. But he still hadn't come to terms with his fatal flaw as a businessman. Practically as soon as the bottles of champagne were drained, he launched straight into what was sure to be the greatest scheme of all time. He bought a small, undeveloped lake in the southern Adirondack mountains and hired a team of architects to draw up plans for a summer vacation community, complete with an 18-hole golf course. It was something there were very few of in that neck of the woods.

But for good reason, because the property was located just inside the Adirondack Park. The park had been dedicated by Teddy Roosevelt in 1892 as a state park, even though it's bigger than all the national parks in America put together. It's an unusual setup. Half of the six million acres are privately owned and half belong to the state, and all of them are strictly regulated by the Adirondack Park Agency. Their mission is to keep the public lands as forever wild as possible and also make it difficult for people to further develop the private half. It's even hard for homeowners to get permission to build additions on their houses.

Did Fred scope out the APA regulations beforehand? Ha. The money from the I-95 deals was burning a hole in his pocket, and he cooked up the new project purely on impulse. It was such a brilliant concept, what could go wrong? Besides, he had spent his whole career convincing officials to sign off on his proposals. Hadn't he just sweet-talked John out of prison?

If only Fred had done his homework, he would've known he was in a whole different league now. The APA rejected his permit application outright. Hell would freeze over before they allowed such a big commercial project in an undeveloped part of the park. The fact that he had already paid for the land and spent a bundle on the plans didn't faze agency officials in the least. Plead with us all you want Mr. Shulley, but the answer is still no. Why didn't you check with us first?

It was like Fred had mistakenly bought a worthless tract

of swampland in Florida, and soon he was up to his eyeballs in debt again. And it would turn out to be only the first half of a big double whammy because when April 15th rolled around, he had nothing left to pay the income tax he owed on the I-95 profits. Then when he didn't file a return at all, pretty soon the IRS was hot on his and Mom's trail.

Just as the IRS was about to place a lien on their house and start garnishing mom's paycheck, Mom and Fred decided to go into hiding. Mom quit her job. Fred closed up shop. And somehow they pulled off a quick cash sale of Mom's second dream house.

Fred's rescue of John before all this went down had sparked a temporary thaw in their relationship. After working at the sawmill for a year, John even moved to the small town near Mom and Fred's place. There he went into business for himself again—a legit one this time—and got married to a nice woman named Judy. Every so often, the two couples met in the evening for drinks. John would bring along his guitar sometimes and sing for everyone.

John agreed to let Mom and Fred put the new house that they had bought with the proceeds from the sale of the old one in his name in order to conceal it from the IRS. As fate would have it, suddenly there they were on the Eastern Shore just outside Seaford, Delaware, not far up Route 13 from me.

Mom and Fred had managed to throw the IRS off their scent, but it was still as though they were under house arrest. Neither of them could get a job because it would've revealed their location and exposed their assets, plus they had no friends or acquaintances in the area. So the only time they went out was to go to the supermarket or the liquor store. The house was no dream house either. But it did have a big yard, and Mom planted a vegetable garden with Fred's help. Except that he was no gardener, and her arthritic back severely limited what she could do. The garden never amounted to much.

The two of them were drinking more heavily than ever.

Sam, meanwhile, had graduated from Georgetown University's School of Foreign Service. After that she went back up to Cecil County and got a job and an apartment not far from where she'd finished growing up.

The first time Sam drove down to visit Mom and Fred in their new digs, it suddenly dawned on her that she had a sister living only twenty minutes away. Sam was too young when I still lived at home for her to remember me much. But she had heard enough references over the years to at least make me a mystery figure in her life.

As soon as Sam learned Mom hadn't been back to see me since the first fiasco, that settled it. They were going to pay a visit to Holly Center the very next day.

They showed up carrying a big dollhouse. It was fully furnished and accompanied by a couple of dolls just the right size. Never having had a dollhouse, I wasn't sure what you were supposed to do with one. Dolls were never my thing. So I was way more excited by the two gorgeous handbags they also brought me—Mom still knew my taste to a T.

There was my baby sister all grown up. Sam was so pretty! With her long, auburn hair and freckles on top of freckles, she looked nothing like me. But I didn't care because I had a sister again. A blood one, too, meaning I couldn't lose her like I did Rebecca Yoder.

Every time I glanced at Sam, she was still smiling at me. It was like a hundred Christmases rolled into one!

Mom looked so much older. Her hair was done up nicely and her makeup was fresh, but underneath you could see how worn down she had become. There was no hiding the puffiness and dark circles under her eyes. Also, it seemed like it took a real effort for her to smile.

Mom and Sam wheeled me around the campus, and just like Chris, Sam was overjoyed to see what a special place Holly Center is. We stopped at the canteen for refreshments—of course—and then Sam spent a whole hour coloring with me back at the cottage. She tried mightily to get me to play with the dollhouse, too. It was perfectly fine to look at, but I simply wasn't interested. Art seems like a much better way to express one's creativity.

It didn't feel the same at all this time when Mom told me they were getting ready to leave. I don't know whether it was because I was so glad to see Sam again, or because I had been at Holly Center for eight years and am so happy here, but now I was okay with Mom going. I just hoped it wouldn't be quite so long between visits.

NO SOONER THAN Holly Center had hit its high of 200 residents, it began to shrink like a cotton shirt after you've run it through the dryer a few times. You don't feel the shirt getting smaller right away, but before long it starts feeling a little tight. Then once our numbers had dropped by about 50, the state began consolidating cottages and laying off staff, a process that is ongoing today.

I didn't notice the changes at first because most of the transitioning residents were from the higher-functioning cottages. But soon the resulting budget cuts were making themselves felt everywhere. They shut down the school and the therapy pool. We stopped going on as many outings. And because the volunteer support fell off, too, not as many events took place on campus anymore.

But thank God Operation Teddy Bear keeps on trucking. Pun intended, haha. They just don't have to send over as many big rigs as they used to.

I NEGLECTED TO MENTION that in 1983 I became an aunt when Betsy gave birth to Lily. The family had put down roots in Albany, where Chris continued teaching at his unusual school, and Betsy eventually decided to become a homebirth midwife instead.

What a thrill to have a niece! And for the next several years, the dominoes lined up perfectly for their visits. With Sam living in Wilmington, John and Judy in the little town of North East, MD, Mom and Fred in Seaford, and me here in Salisbury, Betsy and Chris would take a week off during the summer and drive the family down to see us all. Then after Lily turned three and her sister Sarah was born, Betsy and Chris added a week at the beach to their itinerary. That way they could visit everyone on the trip south and then again on the return leg.

This was when they started taking Lily and Sarah to watch the wild ponies on Assateague Island and camping at Shad Landing while the big picnic I mentioned was happening. Then I got to spend the whole day with the girls, which reminded me of the Yoder's with all those little kids running around.

In the meantime, the small business John had started up when he got back from North Carolina was taking off. He was one of the first with the idea of personalizing the foam sleeves that keep a can of beer or soda cold, which were just becoming popular at the time, with funny phrases and promotional logos. Thanks to the bar and restaurant connections from his days with the band, before long he was marketing his Kool Kups up and down the East Coast. He even had corporations and country clubs for customers, and people would buy whole lots of the koozies, I think they're called now, for weddings and family reunions.

John, who could see what dire straits Mom and Fred were in after they had snuck away to Seaford, asked them if they wanted to go in on the business. Itching for something to do and strapped for cash, they gratefully accepted his offer.

No doubt John was still trying to repay Fred for all his help, but my brother was also a naturally generous person. If he had something that you didn't, you could count on him to share it without even having to ask. Like the single mom who waited tables in one of the restaurants where John performed. She had three kids and no money to spend on them one Christmas, so the week before John played Secret Santa. He got a $100 gift card from Walmart and left it at work for her in an unsigned card. He was aware that she was aware that he was barely getting by, too, and he didn't want her to feel embarrassed.

Anyhow, the family partnership went smoothly at first. They put their heads together to come up with more and more clever things to write on the koozies, and Mom and Fred had some good ideas on how to grow the business. With their input, sales picked up even further.

But then—big surprise—Fred got carried away. He went rogue and started cutting deals without consulting John. Unannounced, Fred also hired an advertising firm, which would've required borrowing on the business to pay for their services.

John realized his mistake too late. When he confronted Fred, Fred told him he was overreacting. You have to spend money to make money, you know.

Mom sided with Fred, and to make matters worse her Hatfield and McCoy gene went wild. She refused to speak to John anymore, and the conflict quickly escalated into another family feud.

The situation left such a bad taste in John's mouth that he stopped putting much time and energy into the business and eventually moved on to something else. He bought a franchise to sell those high-tech vacuum cleaners called Rainbow Machines.

THEN MOM FOUND out she was sick. One day while the dentist was cleaning and checking her teeth, he noticed an open sore behind one of Mom's ears. He urged her to see a doctor about it as soon as possible, which she did. Her doctor didn't like what he saw either and ordered a bunch of tests to find out if the sore was a sign of a deeper problem.

The answer came back: cancer. Nearly fifty years of heavy smoking had left Mom with a tumor in her esophagus.

But the oncologist said that if they removed the entire esophagus and did radiation on the surrounding area, then Mom had a puncher's chance of getting better. Which is good news for a family of fighters like us.

A few days after the surgery, Mom went home with Fred to finish recovering and begin her daily radiation treatments at the local hospital. Sam and Chris drove down whenever they could to help out. But alone at home just the two of them the rest of the time, Mom and Fred grew more depressed than ever.

Fred started playing the ponies at OTB to take his mind off his troubles. Maybe the old magic would return, he thought, except that's not usually how it works. He at least managed to stave off his drinking until the end of the day. After that, all bets were off.

Meanwhile, John's relationship with Fred was back in the freezer again. And John was still so mad at Mom that he retaliated by refusing to speak to her either, even though he knew she was dealing with a type of cancer that rarely ends well.

As for me, Mom's illness meant no more visits to Holly

Center. The next time it would be my turn to go see her.

The radiation treatments didn't stop the cancer for long. Mom began having trouble swallowing and dropping weight fast, and Fred got so frightened at the thought of losing her that he became almost useless as a caregiver. Now they needed someone to help take care of him, too.

By this time Sam had moved from an entry-level job at a Honda dealership into a management position with MBNA, the big Wilmington bank that owned Mastercard and was making a killing in the credit card business. It turned out that the founder of the bank was also a Georgetown graduate, as was Sam's boss. Before Sam knew it, she was on the fast track up.

Sam drove down every other weekend to be with Mom and Fred. Even though she was able to assist them financially now, they continued to spiral downward. The sicker Mom got, the more frightened Fred felt. It became a vicious cycle—the more help Mom needed, the less he was able to provide.

So Sam gave up her apartment, bought a small house just outside Wilmington, and moved Mom and Fred in with her. It cut down on expenses and enabled Sam to be around more to support Mom, who immediately began feeling stronger and gaining back some of the weight she'd lost.

One of Sam's promotions at the bank involved the opportunity to move to Atlanta to open a new branch. Fred was much less freaked out by then, so he and Mom told Sam to go for it and not to worry because they would be able to manage on their own. Also, with Wilmington less of a drive, Chris would be able to come down more often.

Mom and Fred held it together pretty well at first. But after Sam had been gone a few months, Fred's anxiety roared back with a vengeance. By Christmastime he was threatening to kill himself.

The cancer picked up its relentless pace, too. Mom was having more and more trouble swallowing and losing her appetite to boot. Soon her weight loss became a real concern again. It finally got so bad that Mom's primary care doctor told her to go to Christiana Hospital to have a feeding tube inserted.

At the risk of getting ahead of myself for the umpteenth time, I can tell you from experience that this procedure is no fun.

After the doctors put in the tube, they started Mom on another round of radiation to try to shrink the tumors at the base of her throat so that she could eat solid food again. It ordinarily would've been an outpatient procedure, but Sam told the doctors how Mom was no longer able to get the proper care at home. Moving into a hospice wasn't an option either because Mom was still in denial about the reality that she was dying. Could they possibly let her remain at Christiana?

Thankfully, Mom was on a special cancer wing where the nurses and doctors were all angels. They liked her so much that they agreed to fudge the paperwork and let her stay put. She was welcome there as long as necessary.

Sam was in such good standing with the bank by then that they agreed to transfer her to their corporate headquarters, which just so happened to be right next door to the hospital.

Then they generously allowed her as much time as she needed to walk over every day and check in on Mom.

Chris's coworkers joined together to cover for him so that he could spend more time with Mom, too, which he began to do as her condition worsened.

I WAS OF COURSE completely oblivious to the fact that Mom's house was now on fire. But then one day, Holly Center received a call from Sam. By then I was in 700, where they had transferred me once I had to use a wheelchair to get around. Sam explained to Mary, the cottage supervisor, that Mom's cancer was taking over and that she had already outlived the doctors' expectations by more than a year. Just like Daddy, she was hanging on to the point where her suffering was becoming acute. Sam asked Mary if there were any way they could bring me up to see Mom one final time. Maybe it would help her let go.

Mary, who is also made from angel stock, said yes without batting an eye. "Just tell me the room number, and we'll be there in the morning."

It was a Saturday, and Chris and Betsy had driven down with the girls the night before to visit for the weekend. With the four of them and Sam already in Mom's room when Mary wheeled me in, we had a mini family reunion right then and there. Mom wasn't having trouble smiling now. She was beaming at the sight of all of us together at the same time. "Lily and Sarah are my little angels," she proudly announced.

Mary parked my chair sideways next to Mom's bed so

that Mom and I could hold hands. Her grin wouldn't quit just like Tommy's, and she kept telling me over and over how much she loved me. I already mentioned that Mom and I aren't big criers, so ours were the only dry eyes in the room.

You know I'm not much for hospitals, but it felt a little like we were in Mom's bedroom. She had been at Christiana for quite a while, and Sam and Betsy had done all sorts of things to make the room feel more like home. There were family photos everywhere and lots of houseplants and flowers. Chris had even set a potted-up tomato bush on the sill beneath Mom's big, sunny window. It was early fall, and a few of the fruit were starting to ripen. The inside of the door and the walls were plastered with Lily and Sarah's artwork—darn, if only I'd known to bring a coloring book and some crayons!

Tucked in next to Mom was a chocolate-brown teddy bear that the girls had brought down for their grandma when she first checked into the hospital. It was all I could do to keep from stuffing that cute little guy into my bag, but Mom clearly needed him more than me.

Mom was spent by mid-afternoon and had drifted off to dreamland. By then big, chocolate-brown Mary had become a member of the family, too, and after hugs and kisses all around, Mary's aide drove us back to Holly Center.

The next time I saw Mom, that same bear would be lying beside her inside a big wooden box.

THE OTHER PIECE of Mom's unfinished business was

John. He still refused to visit her, even though she was starting to fade fast. It was as if all the accumulated pain and loss had hardened his heart against the very person who had brought him into the world in the first place.

And remember what I said about our stubbornness.

Mom never talked about John, or about dying either. Sam and Chris discussed the situation and were pretty sure that Mom's estrangement from John was weighing heavily on her. It might be another thing keeping her from letting go.

Chris would stay with John and Judy when he came down to visit Mom, and he had been delicately probing John about why he was still so upset. He had his reasons, for sure, but Chris sensed that the blowup over the business wasn't the real source of John's feelings. Besides, trying to sort out the conflict seemed pointless in light of Mom's condition.

So Chris decided to try a different tack and just talk to John about John. He asked him without any judgment how he was going to feel if Mom died while he was still holding onto so much resentment toward her. Was he truly going to be okay with never saying goodbye to his own mother?

When John began to soften, Chris told him he wouldn't have to say a word to Mom if he didn't feel like it. Just sit with her for a while and hold her hand. Deep down she knows she's going to die soon, and she's been getting more and more frightened lately. She'll be so relieved to see you again that the feud will be the farthest thing from her mind. What does it matter anymore anyway?

John rode in with Chris the next morning. They made sure to get to the hospital early enough that John wouldn't cross paths with Fred, who by then wasn't able to pull himself together enough to leave the house until the late afternoon. Mom was dozing. While John stood next to her bed taking in the scene with all the tubes and monitors, she stirred and looked up at him.

Her smile could've melted a glacier.

After Chris conveniently slipped out for coffee, John moved a chair next to the bed and sat holding Mom's hand. Neither of them spoke for a long time. They just silently gazed into each other's eyes—this time Mom had tears in hers. Then John gave her a CD with a couple of his solo albums on it, and she asked him to put it in her player and start it going.

John's mellow voice and guitar accompaniment pretty much became a fixture after that. Mom loved bragging to everyone who came into the room that it was her eldest son they were listening to.

Chris had been right. There wasn't much to talk about.

And Sam and Chris were right about Mom needing to bury the hatchet with John. She immediately seemed more at ease and slept quietly for most of the day while she listened to John serenade her with songs he had written over the years.

Mom's doctor said it wouldn't be long, so Chris decided not to go back home to Albany. He stayed on at John's, and each morning he and John visited Mom together. Sam was almost always there, too. On one of her last mornings, Mom was surprisingly alert. She told the three of them she had just dreamed about dying. What happened was she dove into a well and kept swimming downward until she came up on the other side of a beautiful river. Beside it was a meadow filled with wildflowers in a rainbow of colors, where she felt totally at peace.

When Dr. Bakshi heard about the dream, he knew it was time to call all the nurses on the wing into her room. "Mrs. Shulley," he declared, "is now the queen of this ward. I want you lined up outside her door twenty-four-seven so that whenever she needs anything, all she has to do is clap her hands and you will get it for her without a second ticking off the clock. Is that clear?"

The nurses nodded and smiled. Mom, wide awake, started beaming again.

She died two days later, with Chris, having spent the night in her room with her, there holding her hand. It was a few minutes past sunrise.

THREE DAYS AFTER that, Mary, her aide, and I drove up to a beautiful chapel attached to Sam's old elementary school. Betsy and the girls had come down the morning Mom passed, and I met them there. Sam, Chris, John, and Judy had already arrived, too. Fred looked like he should still be in bed. He was a mess.

The chapel was packed with Mom's friends and former neighbors and coworkers. The nuns who had been Sam's teachers were also in attendance. Mom was lying at the foot of the altar in a long, narrow box made of very shiny wood, and Mary pushed me over to it so that I could see Mom up close. She looked so beautiful. Her hair was done to perfection, and the dark circles were gone from under her eyes. There was even the hint of a smile on her face. But her eyes were shut tight, and she was so, so still. Although I felt confused by what I was seeing, somehow I knew it was okay.

And there was that cuddly bear again. Somehow I also knew he was not to be mine, that Mom still needed him to stay with her.

The funeral Mass began, and Sam and Chris took turns at the pulpit reading prayers from the bible. They returned later to tell stories about Mom. Both of them were crying, as was pretty much everyone else. Then the priest, who had known Sam since she was a young girl, talked about Mom going to be with God. He said her pain and suffering had been washed away, and from now on the only thing she would feel would be joy.

All that was left for her to do was to rest in her dream meadow full of flowers.

After they closed the lid on the box, a bunch of strong men carried it out to the equally shiny black car that had been waiting in front of the chapel. It reminded me of Operation Teddy Bear with those football players hoisting us up into the cabs. We followed the car into a large field next to the chapel. While everyone stood around a deep hole in the ground, a machine slowly lowered the box into the hole. The priest said another prayer, and then people took turns throwing flowers and handfuls of dirt on top of the box. There was a lot more crying.

I still didn't understand what was happening, but again I sensed nothing wrong. Little did I know that twenty-five years later I would wind up back in the same field.

SEVEN

In my 35th year on this good earth, which would've made it 1990, JFK and RFK's younger brother Ted took up the Kennedy torch for the developmentally disabled. A very young U.S. senator from Massachusetts, he managed to get Congress to enact something called the Americans with Disabilities Act.

Chris says the legislation is a true civil rights law because in the bill Senator Kennedy wrote, "Historically, society has tended to isolate and segregate individuals with disabilities, and, despite some improvements, such forms of discrimination against individuals with disabilities continue to be a serious and pervasive social problem."

The ADA established legal protection for developmentally and mentally disabled people, which is how it later became the basis for a Supreme Court case known as the Olmstead decision. Chris looked it up, and what had happened was that two women in Georgia named Lois Curtis and Elaine Wilson, both of whom were struggling with mental health issues and intellectual disabilities, ended up being trapped in one of their state's big mental hospitals.

Lois and Elaine had voluntarily checked themselves in because at that point there were still no community-based services available to them. The hospital psychologists determined that with enough support, Lois and Elaine were perfectly capable of living on the outside. But because the support didn't exist, they had no choice except to stay in the hospital. Chris says this is a typical example of conservative southern states refusing to fund social programs—and ignoring civil rights laws, too.

Somehow Lois and Elaine found themselves a Legal Aid attorney and sued the state commissioner of mental health, whose last name was Olmstead. When the case reached the Supreme Court, a majority of the justices ruled that mental illness is a form of disability and found Georgia in violation of the Americans with Disabilities Act. They ordered the state to do whatever it took to enable the two women to get the treatment they needed in a community-based program.

Chris couldn't find out whatever happened to Elaine, but he did learn that Lois's story ended up a lot like Turk's. She lived in a group home for a number of years, where she began to blossom as an artist. And she's been living independently ever since, sharing a beautiful house with a fellow artist in the Stone Mountain area of Georgia.

Lois receives support from a "microboard," a volunteer group of family and friends who collaborate to help disabled individuals manage successfully on their own. It seems to be working out just fine for Lois. At a recent exhibition of her paintings, she auctioned one for $1,400!

But this is where, for me, it gets all tangled up again. In

response to the Olmstead decision, the Civil Rights Division of the Justice Department ordered Georgia to close its state-run mental hospitals and move all mental patients and developmentally disabled residents into privately operated group homes.

It looks like such a good idea at first glance, but a lot of those people weren't like Lois. Many of them had more caretaking needs than group homes could handle. The collateral damage, therefore, was awful—*500* died in the first year alone. It got so bad that the Justice Department had to order the state to halt the transition process until such time as there are enough safe places for everyone to live.

HERE'S A MUCH-CLOSER-TO-HOME example of just how complicated our situation is. Before my cottage mate Ginger—or at least she was until cancer sent me to the infirmary to be closer to Dr. Waris—came to Holly Center, she found herself in a bind that was kind of the opposite of Lois and Elaine's. Ginger's father had to fight for her right to *stay in* a state-run ICF in the Maryland suburbs just outside DC.

Ginger's story is a sad one. She was the only child of an older couple that had put off having children because her father was busy fighting in World War II. It was a dream childhood with a doting mom and dad who saw to it that Ginger had everything. When she got to Wheaton High School, not only was she pretty but an honor-roll student and accomplished pianist, too. Then disaster struck at sixteen.

Out of nowhere she came down with viral encephalitis, and because this was in 1961 when there weren't a lot of treatment options, she wasn't expected to survive at all. By the time her body fought off the virus, it had taken a portion of her brain with it.

Ginger became a lot like me in a matter of days. She entirely lost her ability to speak and was susceptible to seizures at any time. Her mother and father tried taking care of her at home, but Ginger's balance never returned. She was constantly falling and hurting herself. They got her a helmet to protect her head, but after a while they were just too exhausted to go on.

A carpenter by trade, Ginger's father didn't earn enough to cover the cost of private care. The only option was to have her admitted to the 5,000-bed Springfield State Hospital. There she suffered the fate that I somehow managed to avoid, being left to waste away on the back ward of a huge, decrepit asylum.

Ginger got a reprieve in 1970 when the State of Maryland responded to JFK's mandate for the first time and built an ICF in Montgomery County called Great Oaks. It was more than twice the size of Holly Center and not as connected to the community, but it was still a lot nicer than where she had been spending the previous seventeen years. Ginger was able to move right in just like I got to do here.

Her troubles were far from over, however. While she was living at Springfield, she had been forced to fight to protect her food. So when she first arrived at Great Oaks and meals were served, she would get agitated and frantically start waving her hands back and forth above her plate. Which caused the staff to label Ginger "aggressive" and place her on the locked wing with the psychiatric "patients."

Then thank God, an angel came into Ginger's life, too: a staff person at Great Oaks who had grown quite fond of her. Mary had spent enough time on back wards where food shortages were common to surmise that Ginger's mealtime behavior was defensive, not hostile. There was no way Ginger belonged on the psych wing, and Mary was able to convince Ginger's caseworker to move Ginger back in with the other developmentally disabled residents.

But whoever first said that lightning never strikes twice in the same place didn't know what they were talking about. Maryland reacted to the Americans with Disabilities Act just like a bunch of other states by deciding to close *all* its state-run facilities, even the good ICFs, and relocate everyone to private group homes instead. Meanwhile, Ginger's mother had passed away, and in the ensuing three years, her father and Mary became close. Sharing the same concerns about group homes that my family did, Bill and Mary sued to keep Great Oaks open for its high-needs residents.

The lawsuit bought Ginger more time at Great Oaks, but eventually the state succeeded in forcing her out.

Bill and Mary were real fighters. Somehow they managed to get the state to agree to reassign one of Ginger's caregivers at Great Oaks to Ginger's new group home. Ginger was in her early fifties by this time and had become what today they call "medically fragile." Thanks to the aide, who was thoroughly trained and intimately understood Ginger's needs, the transition to the group home went smoothly. Life there wasn't so bad after all.

Can't you just sense another "but" coming? Ginger was one of the home's first residents, *but* as they took on more, the corresponding staff they added was less and less experienced. The group home industry had turned caring for the disabled into an entry-level job, and the low pay was causing a lot of turnover.

Ginger's aide grew worried that they could longer handle someone like Ginger. Her observation was that the staff now consisted mostly of a bunch of glorified babysitters, who sat around with the residents and watched television all day. When the manager brushed off the aide's concerns, in frustration she asked to switch to working nights so that she wouldn't have to be around the unmotivated day shift anymore.

With her former aide no longer there during the day, Ginger's situation went downhill fast. One Saturday morning Mary, who visited Ginger all the time, came in and noticed that Ginger was running a fever. Mary asked the staff about it, and they said that Ginger probably just had the same head cold as one of her housemates. Worried about how hot Ginger's forehead felt, however, Mary pressed further and asked why they hadn't taken Ginger to see a doctor. The answer: "He won't be in until Monday. We're going to take her then."

Mary insisted that they bring Ginger to the emergency room right away. Which was a very good thing, because it turned out what Ginger had was a serious case of pneumonia.

And on top of that it was aspiration pneumonia, meaning that she was somehow breathing food down into her lungs when she ate. Mary got nowhere when she asked the staff why this was happening and how they could prevent it from happening again.

Ginger's health had become so fragile that the next time she got pneumonia might be the last. In the end, Mary and Bill were forced to hire a speech therapist to follow up on the swallow test that they gave Ginger at the hospital. The therapist used the results to draw up a safer diet for Ginger and also taught the group home staff how to monitor her eating habits better.

Another time Ginger somehow wound up with a broken hand, and when Mary asked the staff what had caused it, all she got back was a bunch of shrugs. Her best guess was that someone had yanked Ginger abruptly up out of her wheelchair.

Yet another time, Mary discovered an ugly scrape on Ginger's back. Neither Bill nor Mary were notified of the injury, and when Mary demanded an explanation, once again none was forthcoming. It looked a lot like a rug burn to Mary, leading her to suspect that the same aide who had injured Ginger's hand may have dragged Ginger across the carpet in the dayroom while trying to get her up after a fall.

This is all so amazing to me because at Holly Center, if I so much as scratch my face during one of my outbreaks of itchy dry skin, then they immediately tell Sam or Chris about it. They explain what they're going to do to take care of the problem, too.

Chris's friend who keeps an eye on group homes says this is another major shortcoming. While ICFs like Holly Center have to follow very strict federal regulations, private group homes are governed by state guidelines for reporting illnesses and injuries that are often lax and full of loopholes.

It's worth adding that Mary did a little digging of her own and learned that in the first eighteen months after they shifted everyone from Great Oaks into group homes, *a third of them died.*

That's right folks, you *cannot* make this up.

THE LATEST INJURY was the last straw for Bill and Mary. Fortunately for Ginger, they had sent Mary to observe the newly-opened Holly Center while Mary was working at Great Oaks. It was everything in her eyes that a truly community-based center for developmentally disabled people should be, and now she made up her mind to find a way to get Ginger in. She and Bill relocated to Ocean City so that they would be in the six-county region that Holly Center is mandated to serve. Then they submitted an application on Ginger's behalf.

The trouble was that now the state was doing everything it could think of to shut Holly Center down, too. Fortunately the center had too much local political support to close it outright, which is why I'm still here. But now that the state has managed to close the center to new residents, Chris thinks their strategy is to wait for enough of us to die off and then claim that continuing to fund the center is no longer justified.

Mary and Bill refused to take "No" for an answer when the state denied Ginger's application. Long-time members of VOR, the advocacy organization I mentioned, they reached out to Hugo Dwyer, who said that Ginger's case is a classic example of a person needing a level of care not available in a group home. So VOR found a big law firm willing to take on Ginger's case pro bono. After battling back and forth for years, they finally won a bizarre concession from the Maryland Attorney General. He agreed that Ginger's group home wasn't adequately addressing her needs and that the state should pay for her to go somewhere that would. But with one stipulation—it couldn't be located in the state of Maryland!

They are that determined to starve Holly Center out of existence.

And then the story takes its strangest twist of all. While Mary and Bill were challenging the AG's decision, Ginger suffered another significant injury. Mary had been complaining to the group home director about Ginger not getting to go out enough, and so one day the staff took Ginger along with two other residents to Baltimore to watch a housemate practice for the Special Olympics. As they were raising Ginger back up in the van's wheelchair lift for the return trip, her big toe got caught between the threshold of the van door and the steel lift platform. Ginger screamed out in pain. But by the time they stopped the lift, her toe had nearly been severed.

The accident amounted to gross negligence. First, the staff failed to put the footrests on Ginger's wheelchair before they left the group home. Also, because they forgot Ginger's shoes, she was only wearing socks at the time. Then the aide operating the lift didn't notice that Ginger had slid so far down in her chair that her foot was dangling dangerously close to the gap between the lift platform and the van.

Although the staff did notify Mary this time, they still proceeded to underreact yet again to a potentially life-threatening situation. They had Ginger's toe examined at the nearest urgent care clinic, where Mary rushed over to support Ginger. When the doctor removed Ginger's blood-soaked sock and saw the severity of the wound, he told them he didn't have the skills to do what needed to be done. She should be seen by an emergency room physician right away.

It's a good thing that Mary was present because when Mary told the staff she would meet them at the ER, they said that they would first have to take the everyone back to the group home for lunch. Mary went ballistic. She jumped into the van with the others and demanded that they drive Ginger and her straight to the nearest hospital.

After they dropped Ginger and Mary off at the entrance, it was two and a half hours before anyone from the group home came back to see how Ginger was doing.

The pain became so excruciating while Ginger was waiting to be examined that she started having seizures. Thankfully they were able to stabilize her enough for an orthopedic surgeon to successfully reattach Ginger's toe before it was too late. Then, concerned about the threat of infection, he kept her in the hospital and started her on a round of powerful IV antibiotics.

This time at least, Ginger's ordeal had a silver lining. Mary took her outrage over the accident straight to the news media, and the following day she demanded that the state agency responsible for regulating group homes conduct a thorough investigation.

Not long after, Mary's attorney—Bill had passed away in 2005—received a call from the AG's office. If Mary agreed to back off, the state would finally allow Holly Center to admit Ginger.

It had been eight years since Mary and Bill first put in the application.

This is how Ginger came to reside with me in 700. Given that she was 68 by that point, it wasn't a day too soon. She loves it here every bit as much as I do. And boy does she get around. Mary lives only 40 minutes away, and so Ginger goes over to Ocean City all the time to visit. Mary even bought Ginger a motorized wheelchair with big, balloon tires so that they can hang out on the beach. This way Ginger gets to dip her poor toe that got so badly mangled into the Atlantic Ocean every once in a while.

Imagine how good it must feel.

CHRIS SAYS OUR situation is ironic because the whole point of a civil rights movement is to give people with a history of oppression *more* choices and options than before, not *fewer*. But with the government's new policy of shutting down *all* state-run residential facilities for the developmentally disabled, we're about to be left with group homes as our only alternative. And when they finish closing the sheltered workshops, too, the only place we'll be able to work will be out in the mainstream. What realistic opportunities will that leave for people like Ginger and me?

It wasn't supposed to turn out like this. Chris also learned from Hugo Dwyer that the justices in the Olmstead decision specifically declared that privatized group homes *should not* be forced on us. They recognized the reality of highly vulnerable people needing to have ongoing access to ICFs like Holly Center.

Justice Ruth Bader Ginsburg made it very clear. "For some individuals, no placement outside the institution may ever be appropriate," she wrote in the majority opinion. "Some individuals, whether mentally retarded or mentally ill, are not prepared at particular times—perhaps in the short run, perhaps in the long run—for the risks and exposure of the less protective environment of community settings; for these persons, institutional settings are needed and must remain available."

So why is our government ignoring her?

While Chris was doing his digging, he also found out that the same thing has been happening to the mentally ill for whom the state hospitals were intended in the first place. Congress has consistently refused to allocate enough money for the programs and services they need to manage elsewhere.

In 1980 President Carter somehow persuaded Congress to increase mental health funding, and the situation briefly improved. But then Ronald Reagan followed right behind him and repealed the Carter legislation. Reagan convinced

Congress to end the federal government's role in providing services to the mentally ill altogether. From there forward the government would give the money to individual states and leave it up to them to deal with the problem.

But right off the bat, naturally, Congress reduced the total number of dollars by *30%*.

And we saw what states like Georgia decided to do with their share of the pie, which was basically nothing at all. And which was why Lois and Elaine ended up having to sue them.

By 1985 federal funding had dropped all the way down to *11%* of local mental health agency budgets. Still, the so-called "deinstitutionalization" of the mentally ill continued to pick up speed. And what has been happening to the people who can't function on their own without outside support? Their newfound "freedom" and "inclusion in society" either leads to homelessness or jail.

It's hard to imagine them being worse off than they were before, but that is exactly what has come to pass—in the name of making government smaller and keeping it from intruding into people's lives.

Sound familiar?

But actually, according to Chris, it's all about the money. He found out that it costs almost four times more to care for us in places like Holly Center, where we get the care we need, than it does in group homes where we don't. Which he says reminds him of the old French saying, "The more things change, the more they stay the same."

If you're not quite sure what that means, just ask someone like Ginger who was once locked inside a state hospital.

EIGHT

Soon after Mom died, Sam got another promotion at the bank. This one involved sending her to Cleveland to open up a new branch. Fred was still an emotional wreck—though at the advice of his doctor, he had stopped drinking—and so Sam took him with her and found an apartment big enough for them both. Fred joined a gym, started working out every day, and gradually pulled himself together. Who thought he would outlive Mom like this?

Chris and Betsy continued bringing the kids down to the beach every summer and stopping to see me along the way. Lily and Sarah were growing up fast! They were both such sweet girls and so intelligent, too. I bet Ginger was a lot like them at that age. I only wish they lived closer so that I could've seen them more often. Their visits always made my day.

In 1994 John and Judy moved to Hawaii so that Judy could be near her only son who was stationed at Pearl Harbor. Then, when Judy followed Jason back to Maryland after his hitch in the Navy was up, John made up his mind to stay put. He said it had always been his dream to settle in the Islands.

After Judy had gone, John decided to move from Oahu to Kauai because he had heard it's even more beautiful there. He ended up loving it so much that he didn't want to go anywhere after that. The only times he left were for Sam's wedding in '99, and then a few years later when he hopped over to the Big Island with Betsy and Chris to watch the volcano erupting.

Sam and Fred spent four years in Cleveland. When Sam returned to the corporate offices in Wilmington, Fred was stable enough to live on his own again. It's so interesting that they both fell in love after they got back—Sam with a coworker named Howard and Fred with a woman also named Judy, who was living in the same apartment complex.

Howard was pretty far up the ladder at the bank, as was Sam by this time. For their wedding they took over a whole wing of the Hotel du Pont. MBNA was then the largest credit card bank in the world, and the president and the CEO both came with their wives, meaning it was quite the elegant affair. Sam even rented tuxes for our two hippie brothers, who by all accounts blended in nicely. Because it was so formal that kids weren't invited, I was more than happy to sit that party out.

After that, Sam would occasionally bring Howard along when she came to visit me. He's a very nice guy, and I could tell the two of them are quite happy together.

Fred, it turned out, had already tied the knot with Judy a few months earlier. Isn't it interesting that he didn't tell Sam about it until she invited him to her wedding?

It also turned out that Mom had made Fred promise

to play Santa for me at Christmastime. So after he and Judy were married, he started doing exactly that. It was Judy who did the shopping and wrapped the presents. Then Fred would drive her down and wait in the car while she delivered them and stayed for a little visit. It was always lovely to see her. As for Fred, I'm all for the idea that it's the thought that counts.

Once John had gotten himself established on Kauai, he came up with the idea of opening a little restaurant. Howard liked John's concept of one that would cater both to locals and tourists, and so he agreed to finance the remodeling and other start-up costs. Because the location had previously been a grungy, Chinese take-out place, John had to work like a dog to make it a cozy spot to sit down and eat. An artist friend of his named Lana turned one whole wall into a beautiful mural of the Pacific Ocean in exchange for a lifetime of free meals.

But the timing couldn't have been worse. A couple of weeks after John welcomed the first customers to the Surf and Turf Cafe, terrorists crashed two passenger jets into the World Trade Center and another into the Pentagon. Not a single plane flew to Hawaii for the next several weeks, and the tourist business died altogether. It would take years for it to fully recover.

The restaurant, as a result, got off to a miserable start. The bills were piling up fast, and John wasn't bringing in nearly enough to cover them. He reached out in desperation to Howard about extending the financing until business on the island picked up again. An astute businessman, Howard didn't like the look of things. He told John it was too risky to go farther into debt—better to cut your losses now than to dig yourself a hole so deep you might never get out.

This felt to John like yet another family betrayal, and thus a new feud was born. Poor Sam was caught in the middle again, just as she had been between her parents and John.

John was determined to keep the place going. He renegotiated his lease with the landlord, who had been watching storefronts go vacant all over the island and was happy just to have his building stay occupied. Then John let the chef go and did all the cooking himself. On top of that, he cut his personal expenses way down by moving out of the house he'd been renting and into a garage for $200 a month.

Talk about family stubbornness—somehow John managed to keep the doors to the cafe open for another five years.

MEANWHILE, LIFE at Holly Center remained pretty much business as usual. Other than my move to 700, along with the closing of more cottages as our numbers continued to shrink, nothing much changed around here. As I mentioned, Holly Center is considered such a prime job that the same staff keeps coming back year after year. The one thing that *was* changing, however, was the residents. Those of us who were still here were slowly growing old together. It would be fun to compare pictures from when we first arrived with ones taken now, nearly thirty years later.

Thankfully there was still no talk of closing Somerset, so I got to continue enjoying my days there and the daily bus ride back and forth.

Except for the hip surgery, which was very straightforward, and an occasional cold, my health was steady as she goes. Chris would always say it was because there's been so little stress in my life since I came to Holly Center, which was also why I didn't have any gray hair. That always made him so jealous.

But then as I eased into my mid-50s—still with fewer gray hairs than you could count on both hands—a nagging sore spot developed deep in my middle. Barely noticeable at first, it kept getting a little worse every day. Now I wasn't scratching my face because it itched, but because one of my kidneys was starting to ache. The staff kept rubbing special lotion into my skin and wondering why it wasn't helping this time.

I was also only picking at my food, which as you know isn't like me at all. Or I would put something tasty in my mouth and then only chew it partway without swallowing. Dr. Waris told Sam and Chris that this sometimes happens to profoundly disabled people as they age. For some reason, we can lose the instinct to complete the eating process.

Then one day my appetite vanished entirely. Even though the staff kept trotting out my most irresistible faves, I just wasn't interested anymore. Dr. Waris rightly sensed something must be *very* wrong. He checked me into the local hospital so that they could run some tests and try to locate the source of the problem. And since I was losing weight so rapidly, he said they'd better put in a feeding tube until they figured things out.

There I was back in my least favorite place of all.

Thankfully, my Mary sat with me during the day to keep me from worrying too much. The nurses gave me awful, chalky things to drink, and then the doctors took pictures of my insides. Finally, after several annoying days of poking and prodding and scanning, Dr. Waris pointed to one of the images. "There it is—it's her right kidney," he said. "It's too badly infected to treat with medication and will have to be removed."

Dr. Waris referred me to a kidney specialist at the University of Maryland Hospital in Baltimore. There wouldn't be any quick in and out this time. First they wanted to give me IV antibiotics to calm down the infection, then do the surgery, and then keep me around until they were sure my digestion was working again.

Sam and Chris took turns coming down to be with me. They stayed in nearby hotels, and I got to see much more of them than usual. The other good news was that it meant new pocketbooks and teddy bears, which definitely took the edge off my misery. But there was always someone barging into my room to do something to me, and the doctors and nurses were complete strangers. Plus I couldn't even remember the last time I had been able to work at Somerset.

The operation was a success, and my other kidney looked perfectly fine. But I had already been having trouble with the canned nutrition they were giving me through the feeding tube. Something about it made me sick to my stomach, making it very hard to keep down. Meanwhile, I didn't have any extra pounds on me to begin with and was continuing to lose weight. So the kidney doctor told Dr. Waris he wasn't willing to discharge me until I stopped vomiting and started gaining again.

Given that I had already been throwing up my food at Holly Center, how was keeping me cooped up in a hospital I hated going to help? Days went by and nothing changed. Even though everyone was being very kind, I began to feel like I was back in limbo again.

Chris thankfully was able to read the situation and figure out what to do. No doubt he was getting tired of his cheap hotel and couldn't wait to get back to Betsy and the girls. He phoned Dr. Waris and asked, "Don't you think Susan will be more likely to start tolerating the tube feeding if she's home with her people and sleeping in her own bed?" Dr. Waris agreed but said his hands were tied. "The kidney specialist is calling the shots for now."

Lucky for me that Chris is so good at talking people into things. He started by telling the nurses all about Holly Center, how long I have lived here, and why I love it so much. To which he added that it seemed like the stress of remaining in the hospital, where I was clearly uncomfortable, was only going to make my eating problem worse. They thought so, too, and the head nurse said she would speak to the doctor the next time she saw him.

Chris was with me when the doctor came in the next morning, the nurse already having softened him up as promised. He agreed almost immediately when Chris asked if he would consider letting Dr. Waris help me adjust to the tube feeding at home. "Since everything else is normal, I suppose we can give it a try. But Susan will have to come back if she doesn't start keeping her food down soon."

Chris telephoned Holly Center with the good news. Mary had been calling every day to ask, "When can I get my Sue-Sue back?" By the following afternoon, I was resting comfortably in the room next to Dr. Waris's office in the infirmary.

Beyond relief to be out of that hospital, I couldn't wait to get back to work. I kept puking my brains out, however, and soon there was talk of returning me to Baltimore. But Dr. Waris was determined to resolve the issue here. He tried giving me every brand of canned nutrition he could get his hands on, as well as tinkering with the rate that the feeding machine pumped it into my stomach. Finally, he found just the right combination. The vomiting stopped on a dime.

Before I knew it, I was approaching my old fighting weight and back on the bus to Somerset.

Dr. Waris told the staff it was fine for me to go back to solid food if I wanted and to offer me things from time to time to see if there was any desire. But the funny thing was I didn't miss it at all. Maybe I just never felt hungry because the canned nutrition contained everything I needed.

Then one day about a year later, there I was sitting next to Tommy while he wolfed down a big helping of lasagna, and a light bulb went off inside my head. Mary noticed me starting to grunt the way I sometimes do when I want something badly. "Does that lasagna look good to you today Miss Sue-Sue? Wanna try some?"

"GRUNT." It was so heavenly I ate the whole piece. The next morning, the scrambled eggs with sausage smelled pretty tempting, too. Everyone was mystified by the sudden turnaround, which meant no more machine feeding for me.

Life was *really* good again.

I'M SO GRATEFUL for living long enough to become a great-aunt. In 2013, the year after Ginger moved in, Lily and David had Eleanor. Lily had known David since they were kids at a summer camp in Massachusetts. A few years older, he at one point was one of her counselors. They were counselors together when Lily turned 15 and then lost touch once David went off to college. But after Lily graduated from Northeastern and showed up at her first teaching job in New York City, there was David! Unbeknownst to her, he had been hired at the same time.

They just had to fall in love after that little stroke of fate, which is how I came to have my first grandniece. She is named after two people, one of Lily's best friends from childhood, and Eleanor Roosevelt, a childhood hero.

Two years later, Sarah and Joe had Annalise. They had started dating in high school and somehow managed to keep the relationship going while they attended different colleges. Annalise was born with auburn hair just like Sam's. Because Joe is from a devout Jewish family, Sarah decided to convert to Judaism before they got married. Then they named Annalise after Anne Frank, whose full name was Annalise.

Eleanor's little sister Lucy came a year after that. She's named after my great-aunt, who was quite a character. Aunt Lucille was always the first one dancing on the table at the family weddings I told you about. You'd swear that her great-grandniece has the same gravelly, mischievous chuckle.

There's a recent photo of Annalise and Lucy and their moms sitting with me in the foyer of 700. In it, I'm wearing as proud and as pleased a smile as you'll ever want to see.

Susan with (left to right) Lily, Lucy, Sarah, and Annalise.

But just as the new generation was coming in over the threshold, the previous one was on its way out. After his restaurant had finally gone under, John put together a solo music act and managed to support himself by performing in clubs and restaurants around the island. He was living his dream again. But at some point he realized he was feeling fatigued all the time, and no matter how much water he drank while he was singing, his throat got so dry it was hard to get through a set.

John initially went to see a holistic doctor, but the herbal treatments and special diet didn't seem to help. Then when John began having trouble swallowing, he checked himself into the hospital for tests. Even though he had never been a smoker like Mom, they found a malignant growth in his esophagus, too.

Chemotherapy gave John another year. Like me, the cancer spread to his liver and couldn't be stopped. So Chris flew out to spend the final month with him and help ease his way. Chris said John went peacefully in his sleep early in the morning, again just like Mom. It was six months after the birth of Eleanor.

Next came Fred's turn. He had practically reinvented himself once he got over his anxiety and grief around losing Mom. Keeping himself fit and healthy, he stayed happily married for a time. But the dependency and depression that had gripped him while Mom was sick came back in spades when he hit 80. Then, after he had worn out his welcome with Judy, Sam helped resettle him in a nice assisted living place just down the road from her.

With Sam visiting almost every day, Fred lasted several more years. He never did come down with anything. Instead, he simply reached a point where he didn't feel as though he had any reason to go on. But talk about stubborn; he hung on for months, constantly complaining to Sam about how long it was taking to die. Then one evening, with Sam at his bedside, he finally managed to give it up.

Sam has a hilarious story about her dad's funeral. His dying wish, he had told her, was to have some of his ashes sprinkled in front of the monument in Arlington Cemetery that honors the Army Airborne unit he had served in. No big deal, Sam thought, *of course* I'll do it.

Then after Fred had passed, the paperwork for his burial at Arlington arrived in the mail. It stated right there in bold print that dividing up a soldier's ashes is strictly forbidden. No ifs, ands, or buts. The Army gets all of you while you're enlisted, I guess, and all that's left of you when you die.

They're so serious about the prohibition that the ashes have to be delivered to the cemetery by the funeral director who oversaw the cremation, not by a member of the family. But Sam, who is *not* a rule-breaker—she goes to Mass almost every day—wasn't about to ignore a solemn promise to her father. Thankfully, the director just so happened to be an old friend. She told him what a pickle she was in over the ashes, and he reluctantly agreed to put a handful in a separate little box for her.

To hear Sam tell it, it was like a drug deal going down on 14th St. She met the funeral director in the cemetery parking lot early on the morning of the funeral, and as they greeted each other, he slipped the illicit box into one of Sam's very sweaty palms.

Sam, in turn, snuck it into her purse—you know how well *I* have *that* move down—and the funeral ceremony proceeded precisely as planned just like they always do at Arlington. She and Howard scurried back to the parking lot as soon as it was over. With Howard at the wheel, they started driving around to find Fred's monument. But little did they realize that the cemetery is the size of a small city. It took them forty-five minutes to finally stumble upon the damn thing, and Sam was certain black helicopters were hovering overhead the whole time.

But they weren't out of the woods yet because there turned out to be a barrier in front of the monument to keep people from getting too close. Practically frozen with fear by that point, Sam ignored what surely must be the thumping of copter blades—or was it her heart pounding inside her chest? She hopped over the barrier and made a mad dash for the monument. Then she hastily dumped out the ashes, raced back to the getaway car, and they sped off toward I-95 like a pair of bank robbers.

NINE

Even with the state letting Holly Center admit Ginger, we were in more danger of closing than ever. By 2014 only four cottages remained occupied, with rumors of further consolidation that would cut us back to three. The alarming news pushed Beth Engberg's brother Mark to organize a campaign to save my home for the past four decades.

Beth had moved in with us in 1984 before you had to blast your way through the door with guns blazing. She was only 16 and super smart, but she'd been born with profound cerebral palsy that kept her from ever being able to walk, talk, or even feed herself. Though she could understand language better than me and had even learned how to communicate things like "yes" and "no" with hand signals.

Beth grew up right here in Salisbury. As a child, she went off to several residential schools where she was always able to fit in well enough. But she would eventually get homesick and convince her mom and dad to bring her back home. They knew all about Holly Center, of course, and finally decided to give it a try.

With someone from her family always visiting,

homesickness never became an issue. But Beth's physical disabilities had left her medically fragile, and over time she lost the ability to eat and needed to be tube-fed. Then in 2004 she came down with a case of pneumonia that she just couldn't fight off.

She died peacefully here in her own bed, just as I'm about to do.

Mark and Mrs. Engberg continued to be big supporters of the center even after Beth passed. They had both joined VOR when the state started trying to force Beth into a group home, and they're still doing whatever they can think of to help us stay open. Mark even got involved in the fight to save another of Maryland's good ICFs, the one where his uncle had been living for a long time. Mark's lawsuit kept it alive for several more years. By the time they finally shut it down in 2008, the uncle had already died. So he didn't get forced into a group home like the others

Mark was instrumental in bringing a young guy named Ethan to Holly Center. Because Ethan was living with his parents up in Howard County outside of Baltimore, Mark had volunteered to become Ethan's local advocate.

Ethan's story is another painful one. He threw violent tantrums as a child that made him a danger to himself, his siblings, and stuff in the house as well. After he'd smashed several televisions, they put the next one inside an unbreakable case. He would also smear his shit everywhere when he was upset and break windows, too. It finally got so bad that his parents moved his bedroom into the basement where there weren't any. Then they started strapping him to his bed at night to keep him from going on any more late-night rampages.

Ethan was able to attend a day school for children with special needs, but it all fell apart when his teacher accused Ethan's parents of sexual abuse. A Department of Social Services investigation found no truth to the allegations. There was a silver lining, however, because it got everyone to pay attention to how awful Ethan's situation had become.

Ethan's parents were finally willing to admit they needed help. But when Ethan's mom Aimee reached out to the local chapter of the ARC, they put her name on some sort of "critical list" and never called back. The special education superintendent from Ethan's school district eventually recommended that Ethan be placed in "therapeutic" foster care, which the parents were initially willing to consider because by that point the whole family was in crisis.

But then the superintendent added that this meant they would probably never get to see Ethan again—so much for that bright idea.

Conditions at home continued to nosedive, leaving Aimee at a total loss. Then Ethan's guardian angel finally got busy. One morning Aimee opened up about her predicament to a coworker, who then told Aimee she had a brother living at Holly Center. The place is a godsend, she said. Aimee visited, saw for herself how true it is, and immediately applied to the state for respite care for Ethan.

She REALLY needed a break.

The state, however, tried to stonewall Aimee. Sick and

tired of being put on hold, she wrote letters to every one of her legislators, which led to her congressman and state senator both intervening on Ethan's behalf. Also, one of the social workers at Holly Center connected Aimee with Mark, who agreed to help, too. The combined pressure at least got Ethan's foot temporarily in the center's door.

The changes in Ethan were nothing short of miraculous. First Dr. Waris focused on Ethan's severe insomnia. He surmised that Ethan was suffering from cluster headaches and that they were a cause of his violent outbursts. Medication helped with both problems, and the staff went right to work loving him and making him feel at home. Soon he was sleeping through the night, the tantrums having virtually disappeared.

Aimee noticed a difference almost immediately, as Ethan began making more eye contact with her than ever before and becoming way more communicative as well. One day Aimee took him out to lunch, something she'd always been afraid to attempt in the past. Then came a weekend trip to Ocean City that they both enjoyed. And whenever she arrived for visits, there was Ethan hanging out with his friends in 300. Never in his 19 years had he been this social.

The catch was that the state had only agreed to short-term care, so Aimee had to go back to the regional Developmental Disabilities Administration office in Salisbury when the meter ran out. She described how Ethan was thriving at Holly Center and pleaded with them to grant him permanent placement. The regional director said absolutely not. There will be no more residential admissions to any ICF in the state of Maryland. Period.

So Aimee appealed to the statewide DDA director in Baltimore. Now she was practically on her knees begging, her eyes brimming with tears. But she still got the same ice-cold, bureaucratic response.

The refusal spurred Mark into action. He gathered a group of local legislators and county officials—all of whom he knew quite well by this time—and together they went straight to the Secretary of the Department of Health and Mental Hygiene, Maryland's top healthcare official. The reason they had to go over the DDA director's head, Mark told Chris, is that the group home industry and privatized support service providers have gained almost total control over DDA policy. They've succeeded in capturing 95% of the DDA budget, and every time they shut down another state-run facility the percentage climbs even higher.

Chris says it's so typical; he calls it the fox guarding the henhouse.

But thanks to the persistence of Aimee, Mark, and the others, today Ethan is a full-fledged member of the Holly Center family. He participates in all our social events and has a full-time job at Somerset, too. He's a happy and productive young adult with a life worth living.

It's no wonder Mark is so determined to keep Holly Center from becoming the 10th of Maryland's 11 ICFs to shut down. He has a front-row seat for witnessing how incredibly urgent the need remains.

ONE DAY, MARK organized a silent protest out front on Snow Hill Rd. He and a dozen other supporters made big signs that said things like "PROTECT HOLLY CENTER RESIDENTS" and "MARYLAND MUST OFFER CHOICE," and Mark carefully explained our predicament when the media showed up. He told them that group homes are a good option for the majority of developmentally disabled people in the state. However, the three to five percent who are profoundly disabled, medically fragile, or emotionally challenged like Ethan will never be able to manage without the comprehensive range of care that you get in an ICF like Holly Center. We're going to suffer from all sorts of unforeseen complications if the state forces us into group homes.

Chris can attest to what a growing problem this has become all around the country. Just the other day he came across a long article in a newspaper from Chicago, where a team of investigative reporters found that over the previous six years in Illinois more than 1,300 developmentally disabled people suffered injury or neglect in private group homes.

The reporters had to do some serious digging for their information because not only has Illinois *not* been requiring group home operators to report every case of injury or abuse, it *has* been insisting that they sign a loyalty pledge stating they won't say anything that could undermine the governor's plan to close every state-run facility and transfer people into group homes instead.

Just like Mary, Bill, and Mark had to do, the parents of the residents of one of the good ICFs still operating in Illinois are currently suing the state to keep it open. The Murray Developmental Center sounds a lot like Holly Center, with a gym, pool, and nice campus for picnics and special events. But according to those Chicago reporters, this isn't what a spokesman for the ARC is saying. He's telling anyone who will listen that the residents of Murray are "incarcerated" and need to be "set free."

Hmmm.

Mark's efforts here in Salisbury are once again gaining the attention of state and local officials, who are helping to put even more pressure on the government to stop strangling Holly Center. So far the campaign has been a pretty big success. The state has committed to keeping the fourth cottage open and also to making some long-overdue repairs and improvements. They even promised to reopen the therapy pool, which closed years ago during one of the rounds of budget cuts.

The Secretary of Health and Mental Hygiene recently gave a speech about "reimagining" Holly Center, whatever that means exactly. He talked about finding new uses for our unoccupied offices and buildings—except that some of the tenants would be from state agencies with entirely unrelated missions. In the end he was pretty vague on details.

What Mark, Mary Reese, and others would like to see is for Holly Center to expand its role again. They say there are almost 8,000 people with developmental disabilities in urgent need of support services on a statewide waiting list, at least several hundred of them within Holly Center's reach.

Which sounds like a pretty long wait.

Mark and Mary want to turn our unused space into a community resource center that would do things like provide a lot more respite care than we have for a long time. These days the state is only willing to approve it in extreme emergencies like Ethan's, and as we have seen, not without a huge fight either. Mark says the DDA is afraid our respite guests won't want to leave, which of course is exactly what happened with Ethan.

All the state is doing right now, Mark fears, is putting on fresh lipstick until the storm passes. It continues to do nothing to promote what Holly Center has to offer, and our aging population leaves our future very much in doubt.

The resource center could also provide outpatient medical, therapeutic, and dental services. Dentistry is a huge unmet need among the developmentally disabled. We could serve as a training site for students who want to go into the developmental disability field. And we could make recreational opportunities available to people who don't live on campus.

There's no reason why Holly Center shouldn't be buzzing with activity just like it was 25 years ago before the state started putting the squeeze on us.

But Mark says that the ARC and similar organizations like Disability Rights Maryland are continuing to lobby hard against the center's existence. They refuse to let up on their self-serving agenda to make sure that privatized services are the only ones available to us.

Seriously, how do those people sleep at night?

The way Chris sees it, we're becoming a country more

and more dominated by greed. He says that, as we speak, our current Republican president is pulling the same fast one that Ronald Reagan pulled back in the '80s. They're going to slash taxes for the rich again, and then use the exploding deficit that will immediately ensue as an excuse to cut back even further on support for society's most vulnerable.

AT LEAST SAM and Chris can quit worrying about what to do if I were to outlive Holly Center. Thanks to all our dedicated and feisty supporters, finding me someplace else to call home won't be a bridge that Sam and Chris will have to cross.

I don't want to even try to imagine what the rest of my life would've been like if my guardian angel hadn't helped me get here. There's so much I'm going to miss—my friends, the job at Somerset, Mary and Connie and Lisa and Erin, the dances, the parties, the picnics, the trips out on the town. Never a dull moment!

And yeah, Operation Teddy Bear. It doesn't look like I'm going to make it to the upcoming one. But the first thing I won't be around for, it turns out, will be the celebration of Ginger's fifth anniversary at Holly Center. Mary Reese told Chris they're even planning to bring in a rock and roll band in honor of Ginger's love for shaking it loose on the dance floor before she got sick.

I so hate to miss a good party.

Still, it's time for me to count my blessings. Even though things got off to such a rocky start, I wound up becoming one of the lucky profoundly disabled adults with a place to live where every single need is lovingly attended to twenty-four hours a day, seven days a week. And where not a day goes by when you're not appreciated for being exactly who you are.

Here I go wondering about Bill Gates again: Will he be able to say the same thing when all is said and done?

I know Sam and Chris didn't get to visit me as often as they'd wished, but they've spent enough time with me to see for themselves that I'm not exaggerating. Holly Center has truly been as close to heaven on earth as someone like me can ever hope to get.

But what about all the others who haven't been so lucky? The reality, with thousands of us languishing in group homes and the government closing down on our other options, is that we're no better off than we were 50 years ago. The fact that we're not as hidden away anymore didn't do Ginger and Ethan much good until they finally made it to Holly Center, did it?

I guess *my* dying wish is for Ginger, and Ethan, and Jamie, and Tommy, and Vanessa, and all the others never to have to cross that bridge either. I also pray that the center continues to be available to the next generation of Gingers and Ethans, because you know there's going to be one. It's not as though damaged brains and disabling birth defects are going to magically disappear one day.

Then what about the generation after that?

TEN

'm very near the end now. My liver is still pain-free, but the tumor has grown so large that it's pressing upward against my diaphragm and making it harder and harder to breathe. So the other day Dr. Waris ordered oxygen. It keeps me from feeling out of breath and helps keep me calm. Still, the effort it takes to refill my lungs is exhausting. And given how long it's been since I last had any nourishment, my energy reserves are just about spent. I'm starting to look as thin as Daddy got to be.

For a while I clung to the notion of getting dressed and riding the bus to work one last time, but the mere thought of it tired me out even more. Stubbornness can only carry you so far. All I want to do at this point is sleep.

Daddy had trouble letting go because he wanted to stick around for us kids.

Mom struggled with unfinished business and some pretty heavy regrets.

When John was dying, his main concern became what happens to us after we die. He and Chris spent a lot of time at the hospice puzzling over the answer.

Then one morning, very near John's end, Chris found himself being greeted by a big grin the moment he entered John's room. "They told me last night while I was sleeping!" John blurted out. "Now I know what's next!"

"Wow," replied Chris, "but who are *they*, and what did *they* say?"

John's smile widened even further. "Sorry, they said it's a secret—you'll have to find out for yourself when your time comes." Then he closed his eyes and went back to sleep.

Well, I don't have any children of my own to worry about. And since my grandnieces have all been to visit recently, I know firsthand what good hands they're in.

I honestly can't think of a single regret. My life has been as human and complete as anyone else's. Initially, for that matter, it was downright typical. My mother and father were madly in love, and I was the fruit of their joyful union. I was born at the Columbia Hospital for Women like countless other babies, my delivery uneventful. Daddy was ecstatic when the obstetrician announced I was the girl Daddy had so hoped they would have. Mom cradled and nursed me as all mothers do. I fussed when I was hungry or my diaper was dirty and laughed when Daddy tickled me. I got baptized like all the other babies in St. Camillus parish, in a pretty white dress all bordered with lace.

It would end up being the last sacrament I received, however, until the other day when Sam asked a local priest to come and administer the Last Rites. I didn't understand much of what he was doing, plus it felt so odd seeing a priest outside of church.

Then like every child I learned to crawl and after that to walk. My physical anomalies made both skills much more challenging, but learn them I did. And later I matured into a woman just like all girls do. Since then, as you know, I have expressed my femininity in whatever classic ways that I could.

And like all of us, my time is going to run out.

The similarities for the most part end there. On the human spectrum, with all its amazing diversity, I'm more different than most. My neurological incapacity for language has kept me from using words to construct thoughts and ideas. Which has made sharing my inner experience with others extremely hard. My brain is unable to form the images to imagine with. And I've never gotten to venture out and explore the world on my terms.

But none of this stopped me from applying the abilities I do have toward living each day the best I knew how. I didn't take a single one off. And just like so many of my ancestors, I stood right back up every time life knocked me flat. Until now, that is.

What is there to possibly regret after living all these wonderful years in a close-knit, caring community and getting to do work that I truly enjoyed?

Sure, I swiped a few things here and there, but I always gave back what I took. If I could say the words "I'm sorry," I would have.

As for what happens next, I still can't get the part of the brain that shifts thinking into forward and reverse into gear. Those neurons never started firing in the first place. So there's no way for me to ponder a time when I will no longer be here.

What I've always been sure of is how I'm doing right now. And right now my liver can't do *its* job anymore either. Because the cancer has clogged all the ducts, my bloodstream is gradually filling up with the toxins the liver is designed to filter out.

Chris also says you can't live without your liver, haha. Corny jokes are one more thing that runs in the family. Yeah, even at moments like this. Mom was cracking them right up to the end, like the one about the new organization called DAM—Mothers Against Dyslexia. Get it? She told that one to Chris because he was a reading teacher at the time.

THE TOXINS ARE dulling my senses and clouding my mind. It's like being lost in dense fog, so mostly I just sleep. For a while it was the right-beneath-the-surface kind. When the nurse announced she was going to take my blood pressure or clean me and check for bed sores, I would open my eyes and grow alert again. The same thing would happen when visitors came in.

Now I'm so deep-down submerged that I can't seem to reach the surface no matter how hard I try. The interval between breaths is growing steadily longer, too. Every so often enough time goes by that, if you were in the room with me, you'd swear it was my last gasp. But then my body fights to take another one. G-A-S-P.

Next month, when Sam and Chris can make the drive

down, there's going to be a memorial service for me in our auditorium. The whole community will gather to celebrate a life well-lived in this miraculous place. Erin will put together a slide show of all the high points, as is the tradition. That's how they roll at Holly Center—even your legacy receives the best possible care.

Who needs that Gates guy's money anyway?

Which reminds me to mention that, ironic as it may sound, I know a little something about independent wealth, too. You see, all along I have continued to receive monthly checks from Social Security, Civil Service, and the Veterans Administration. Plus there was my biweekly paycheck from Somerset. And because I don't have any expenses to speak of, the money just keeps piling up. There's a credit card for me that Sam can use on shopping sprees when she comes to visit, but what do I ever really need?

If I'd been in a position to invest my income in the right places, maybe Bill and I would've done lunch a time or two.

But you know what they say about being able to take it with you.

DR. WARIS AND his head nurse Shellini take turns checking in on me more often now, to make sure I'm not in distress. The flood of visitors seems to have finally run its course. On some level, I must realize that *they* were all coming to say goodbye to *me* because *they* aren't the ones who are going somewhere. But there's no distress because I know how loved and cared for I am, and here I lie snug in my own bed.

When Mom was dying, Sam bought two plots in the little cemetery where Mom is now. Sam thought the second one would be for Fred, but then he decided on Arlington instead. So she is giving his spot to me.

It seems so fitting, doesn't it? With Fred no longer between us, Mom and I will get to spend the rest of time together. Side by side.

Amen.

SOMEWHERE IN THE background, music is softly playing.

It's time for me to go.